26 Grains

ALEX HELY-HUTCHINSON

26 Grains

100 recipes that use wholesome grains – from energising breakfast porridges to delicious dinners

◼ SQUARE PEG

Introduction

26 grains

Everyone has a story about porridge. I frequently hear tales of how people like theirs, which toppings they prefer, the bowl they make it in, or who made it for them in the past, and where – a lot of ritual surrounds porridge. It's the ultimate nostalgia food because it has been cooked at home as part of day-to-day life almost forever.

Like many, my porridge story began with my mum. Hers was a simple affair: watery oats, a sprinkling of brown sugar and a splash of milk, but with a large family of five kids to feed this was the perfect breakfast for hungry mouths. But, in truth, when I was younger, my dream wasn't a life in food. Growing up, the one area I excelled in was cleaning. My passion was so strong I had frequent territorial battles for the vacuum cleaner with my older sister (the photographer for this book). These went on until the day when, mid-fight, she suckered the vacuum nozzle right onto my head and I lost a perfect circle of hair right on the crown. That day I realised I wasn't cut out for a life of cleaning and so began my embrace of the chaos of the kitchen. But it was years later, after a year abroad in Copenhagen as a part of my degree, that my love affair with porridge really took off.

Living in Denmark was one of the most special times of my life. Pockets of sunshine would draw out crowds of Danes, fully cherishing each last ray. The quiet pace of the bicycles, undisturbed in their own lanes, set the daily rhythm of the city. Instead of lovers locking hands while walking, cycling couples would hold hands side by side. Cheeks would flush a light rusty orange, different from the English rosy red. The Danes are masters of baking and wafts of freshly baked bread and pastries would assail you as you made your way around town. I loved it there; it made such an impression on me. And what struck me most was the quality of life, particularly when it came to food. The tiniest coffee shops, with the most limited of menus, would deliver seemingly effortlessly delicious and creative food. Each day presented

a dilemma: return to a place where I'd had an exceptional experience or try a new restaurant – always welcoming, unique in style, and invariably utterly delicious.

After a few weeks in Copenhagen, I came across a new term, *hygge*. This Danish word has no literal English translation, but evokes feelings of warmth, cosiness and comfort. It was everything I associated with Danish food in general, and in particular the sensation of wrapping my hands around a steaming bowl of porridge. The Danes do porridge properly. As well as oats they use ancient grains like spelt and barley, and top it with fragrant Nordic spices and fresh fruits. A bowl of grains may seem like simple fare but the Danes, wisely, never underestimate it. It is exciting to pair the unique texture and taste of a particular grain with appropriate spices, milks and toppings, thinking about sweet versus savoury, and creamy versus crunchy elements. I now build every porridge recipe according to these principles. And I will forever associate *hygge* with my memories of food in Copenhagen, even as it takes on new inflections for me as I cook today.

When I got back to the UK I couldn't stop thinking about the Danish approach to eating. I wanted to work in food but only for a company with the right ethos when it came to quality ingredients and well-produced food. After graduating I started working at Rude Health, and my bosses there were an inspiration. They encouraged me to demand more from food and to understand how eating well can make you feel better. I realised that what I'd intuited in Copenhagen was really just this: simple food, prepared in the best possible way, makes you feel good – and it tastes sensational.

It was during this time that the seed of an idea from Copenhagen began to grow. I decided to start my own business, 26 Grains. 26 being a number I've always felt drawn to, and grains being where I wanted to start; as well as a play on the idea of grains of knowledge. My plan was simply to try out ideas around my own fascination with grains and see if anyone out there was interested too. And it turned out they were. We first opened in July 2014 as a pop-up at Old Street Station, London, a busy commuter thoroughfare. I was apprehensive at the prospect of launching a porridge business mid-summer. But as one customer rightly said: everyone – your mum, your trainer, your nutritionist, the lot – is telling you to eat porridge. And people are returning to it more and more and cooking it at home, but it is still hard to find a good bowl on the go. When you think of the ubiquity of sugary pastries, porridge really doesn't get the space it deserves.

I often tell my co-workers to not worry if something goes wrong, because it has probably already happened to me. Take our first ever stall at Old Street Station: I had rented a tiny kiosk space and, calling on friends and family for design, carpentry and manpower, built a beautiful white-tiled bar with a light cherry wood front, kitted out with a hob, bain marie, fridge and storage shelves. We'd designed it to roll out into the station during the day and store away in the kiosk at night. We had done the planning and building off-site so when our move-in afternoon came, on the eve of our first day trading, we set off to set up shop. With the freshly tiled bar in tow, we slowly wiggled across London through what seemed like the most painfully bumpy roads. Upon arrival, the heavens opened. We lifted the bar from the van, rolled it down the ramp into the station and located our proud little space. Slight problem: our bar was 1cm too wide each side

for its new home. The measurements we'd been given hadn't accounted for an old glass frame fitted from the previous shop. Luckily we found a space under the stairs in the station to store the bar ready to roll out the next day. At dawn on that first Monday of July, we rolled out the bar and set out all our gear: pots, labels, wooden spoons, compotes and, of course, enthusiasm, all at the ready. But our excitement was soon quashed: the hob didn't work. In the end we spent that first day introducing ourselves, outlining what we'd be serving over the month and psyching ourselves up.

Once we got going it was a super month. We had commuters, fitness enthusiasts, techies, foodies and kids – of all ages and nationalities – chatting to us, dancing to our music and eating our food. It was incredible. I'm often asked what has been my biggest achievement starting my own business, and while there have been a number of amazing moments, for me there is nothing better than seeing a face who has spared a few minutes while I make up their breakfast, return the following morning for more.

After nearly a year of events and pop-ups, I set my sights on finding a space to make our own. With the

help of a few incredibly kind people who believed in the concept and generously put inordinate time and energy into finding and negotiating a potential space, I came across an unused shed in the beautiful courtyard of Neal's Yard. The walls were dark and damp, and there was no water or electricity, but a rich history of independent traders and a tight community made me realise that this was the site for us. We pitched to the landlord – a situation I could have never imagined a year before – and thrillingly, they said yes.

Opening the shop felt like a huge leap from our previous pop-ups and I was uncertain quite how many porridges I might sell in the early days. I needed the security to be able to hire a brilliant team and buy the right equipment, so I turned to a crowd-funding platform. After 30 days and 184 unbelievably kind individuals, we hit our target, enabling us to go from pop-up to permanent. 26 Grains is now made up of ten amazingly bright individuals who make it a pleasure to come into work every day. If I don't tell them enough, let me do so now: they mean an enormous amount to me and to the business. I learn from each of them every day and their dedication and support has been the difference between closing after a year or getting this small idea off the ground and looking to grow, as we now are, with a new site in our prospects. Working in the shop alongside them, in a magical pocket of London, has truly been one of the best parts about this whole adventure.

As the months have gone by I have learnt so much about our capabilities, customers and how best to develop our menu and methods. Changing the menu according to the season has sometimes been a challenge. We would have loved to keep our best-selling blueberry porridge on throughout the year, but it quickly became apparent from the quality of the fruit that the season was coming to an end. We adapted and played on winter spices using beetroot, cranberries and apples together to make a wintry compote. We also experimented with blending the grains in our porridge depending on the way they taste and the texture they add. Our lunch and snack menu has expanded, drawing inspiration from a number of different cooking styles to create warming and nourishing recipes. With a new site I hope we'll be able continue this flow of ideas. The more I learn about grains, the more I want to devise new recipes, from porridges to salads, mains and baking.

Writing this book has been a brilliant opportunity to explore my favourite grains in more depth. I feature nine grains in the recipes that follow: hopefully enough to broaden your horizons without overwhelming your store cupboard. I could have written more recipes but what follows are my absolute highlights. Some draw on what I learnt in Copenhagen, others have been guided by how I have felt and what I've craved, both in times of excitement and when I've been entertaining as well as when I'm tired or keen to take my mind away from the bustle of everyday life. Every grain is added to enhance, and I have enjoyed learning just how versatile they are.

Since I began 26 Grains, I have felt overwhelmed by the excitement of starting my own business, but I have also realised how tricky it can be too. I hadn't anticipated how solitary it would be to start something on my own. When I was testing the concept with my first pop-ups, I was painfully conscious of every cost and whether the long-term outcome would be worthwhile. Every pop-up or event, no matter how big or small, tended to get the better of me the night before, as I worried about what was where, the timings, whether things would run smoothly – particularly with such a short time to set up most mornings. I often shared these worries with those around me, but it wasn't the same as having someone completely dedicated and involved in the idea, wanting it to succeed just as much as I did. That said, there are many people who have come so close to that role and given me much more support than I could have asked. I mention the people close to me in the acknowledgements at the back of this book but in some way the people beyond are just as important as my friends and family. The people who walk into the shops, come to the pop-ups, and even simply interact on social media, the people who enjoy the food and the stories behind the grains. Without you I wouldn't be writing this book. My one hope with this book is that people will be able to share the enthusiasm we have at 26 Grains in their own kitchens.

In the meantime I hope to learn from those around me, from the people working at 26 Grains, from eating at wonderful restaurants, cooking food with friends, travelling and just taking everything in. What I have learnt is that food is more than just the flavour. It's an overall feeling, with all the senses engaged: the music you play while you cook, the voices chatting while you prepare the food, the smells in the kitchen

as the onion starts to soften, the table you eat at – inside or out – and, of course, the taste. I remind myself of that feeling of *hygge* and my time in Copenhagen and know that everything I have learnt about food has included the experience, the company, the atmosphere.

So, where would I like to go with this adventure? Training and gaining a better understanding of food. The subject is a funny one; at first it seems like a simple thing to explore, and perhaps at the beginning of this journey part of me was thinking, 'I like the taste of food, I get hungry, so does everyone, therefore food is something to get involved in.' And, in a way, my original rather naïve outlook stands true – food is simple and universal, it is a leveller. At the same time, the more I find out about food, the more I realise there is a long way to go before becoming any kind of master. But then I guess that kind of sums up what a bowl of grains signifies for me – porridge has delicious depths that belie its simplicity.

GRAINS

Grains

For this book I have chosen to focus on grains. I've become fascinated by their different properties, how they're grown, harvested, what soil they've been planted in and in which climates they grow best. Compared to many other foods their many varieties have lasted through history, stored and used in a multitude of ways.

Most whole grains, husks included, can be sprouted, and in doing so, we start fermentation. Removing the husks exposes the softer inner part of the grain. The softness of the grains varies from species to species, as does the composition of germs and proteins, determining whether grains contain components such as gluten, beta-glucan and lysine. The grains can be cooked whole or processed in a number of ways, such as milling, cutting or flaking.

The most crucial part of cooking with grains is to consider the quality of the grains that you choose. A simple bowl of porridge can be made even better both in taste and the way it makes you feel if you choose a lesser known variety of grain, which has been processed the fewest possible number of times. At the shop, we roll our oats ourselves through a flaker, which simply splits the soft oats through two disks, and flattens them so that you can still see the colour of their outer layer and so that all the components of the whole grain remain, nutrients included. It makes for a creamier, more nourishing and sweeter bowl of porridge, setting ours apart from any cut, rolled, steamed quick oat.

Wheat and gluten have become a hot topic of conversation in food. There is no doubt about the efficiency of using genetically modified crops but it has been at the expense of the traditional craft of growing and cooking with certain grains, particularly wheat. Instead, I choose to use the least processed grains that contain gluten, such as spelt, barley and rye – ancient grains that have been unaltered since their original cultivation and which maintain their minerals and nutrients. I have also included a few pseudograins which, like ancient grains, have lasted unchanged throughout history.

All of the grains in the pages that follow have their own unique flavours and their own ways of reacting when cooked or baked – they provide both a challenge and a reward.

Amaranth

ORIGIN

Amaranth is actually a seed, a pseudograin that comes from a tall wilting plant with broad green leaves and bright pink flowers with miniscule little buds.

First grown in ancient Mexico, Guatemala and Peru, amaranth was one of the most popularly consumed foods before the Spanish conquest. In the festival to praise the Aztec god of war, amaranth was toasted like popcorn, mixed with honey or chocolate, made into a statue of the god and then eaten as a treat.

TASTE

Amaranth is a very fine grain that is fairly nutty in flavour. It works well with rich flavours such as chocolate, nuts and spices – think Mexican and South American flavours such as chilli, chocolate, honey, avocado and tomatoes. I use it to make a Spicy Sweet Potato with Amaranth and Ginger Crème Fraîche (see page 167).

Amaranth is most commonly found as a whole or popped grain. The popped grain is great for adding nuttiness to a dish, texture to salads or for making on-the-go granola bars and other treats. You can even pop them yourself in a dry frying pan.

Amaranth can be milled into a flour; however, it can be difficult to bake with as it's incredibly dense. The flour is best used as a gluten-free thickening agent.

NUTRITION

Amaranth is the only grain reported to contain Vitamin C and has also been documented as having the highest level of calcium of any grain.

These grains might be small but they pack a punch with their high levels of Omega-3, manganese, magnesium, iron and selenium. They are also a rich source of protein, as well as the plant protein lysine, which is made up of important amino acids that make it easy for your body to digest the grain and reap its benefits (this is a characteristic of pseudograins). Coeliacs are able to consume these grains as they're free from gluten.

FACT

It's not just the seed that you can eat – in Indian dishes, the leaves are steamed and mashed with salt, chilli and cumin to create a dish called keerai masail. They are also used in stir-fries in China and soups in Vietnam. The white, milky root of a mature amaranth is also a popular part of the plant to cook with, often mixed with tomatoes and tamarind gravy to make a savoury, creamy dish.

Barley

ORIGIN

Barley was one of the first crops to be domesticated for human consumption and today is grown in over 100 different countries. It is a member of the grass family, and each blade of barley is characterised by the number of rows of seeds – six-row barley is the most common. Barley is used throughout the world to make beer, using a process known as sprouting or fermentation, in which moisture stimulates the germination process inside the grain to produce the sugars needed for malting and distilling.

TASTE

Barley has a light nuttiness to it. The texture is somewhat similar to brown rice or oatmeal, even though the grains are larger with a definite chewiness, but tender throughout. It suits both sweet and savoury dishes, including stews, soups, porridges and puddings. Barley contains the gluten protein and is often used in baking.

The most common form of barley available is pearl barley, which is processed to remove the outer husk and bran – it has a strong, earthy flavour and makes a fantastic 'risotto' (see page 157) but don't neglect any other type that you come across, such as barley flakes. Whole barley with the husk gives the best results for sprouting (see page 49).

For additional depth, toast your barley ahead of cooking to make the dish slightly more smoky and buttery. If you have any left over, you can brew the toasted barley to make barley tea, a drink common in Asia (see page 235).

NUTRITION

High in essential nutrients and minerals, including selenium, phosphorus, copper and magnesium, barley is a nourishing whole grain that will help keep your health in balance. It is rich in both soluble and insoluble fibres, meaning that it slows down the absorption of sugar in the body as well as maintaining a healthy bowel. Similar to oats, the germ of the grain contains beta-glucan, proven to maintain and reduce cholesterol levels.

The benefits of barley are made more bioavailable after a period of soaking (see page 48) – remember that as a whole grain, barley will take longer to soak than pseudograins. The ideal soaking time would be 6–8 hours but it will benefit from an even shorter soak time.

FACT

The diet of Roman gladiators was most typically vegetarian with a high proportion of grains and legumes. These gladiators were often referred to as Barley Men, or *Hordearii*, as the consumption of barley was said to improve their stamina and give them more strength.

Buckwheat

ORIGIN

Despite its name, buckwheat is a pseudograin, and not from the same family as wheat. It is, in fact, the seed of a plant related to rhubarb and sorrel, which is why I often pair it with rhubarb (see page 64).

It is thought that its name comes from the Dutch word *bockweit*, which literally means 'beech wheat', since the grain's unusual triangular shape resembles a beech nut and it is used in a similar way to wheat.

TASTE

Many use buckwheat as an alternative to rice or porridge, but be warned: it's not only unique in shape but also in taste. It can sometimes be quite bitter and earthy and the key is to rinse the grain well ahead of cooking to ensure the flavour is fragrant rather than overpowering. The texture is much softer than, say, spelt or barley.

More recently, buckwheat is becoming popular as an alternative grain to bake with, ground into flour and used for breads, pancakes and other goodies (see my recipe for Buckwheat Banana Bread, page 84). In France, buckwheat is used in crêpes and galettes. Other ways to use buckwheat include boiling it to add to salads and soups, or toasting it for a fragrant, nutty crunch.

NUTRITION

Buckwheat is suitable for coeliacs, being completely unrelated to wheat and therefore not containing the gluten protein. Its immune-boosting characteristics include the ability to reduce cholesterol through rich supplies of magnesium, as well as having high levels of zinc, copper and manganese.

It's also a great source of protein and lysine, an amino acid that is important for those following a plant-based diet as well as making the grain easier to digest.

Since buckwheat is a seed it contains flavonoids, plant pigments with phytonutrients that boost the action of vitamin C, both helping the body to fight disease and acting as an antioxidant.

Eating buckwheat also helps control blood sugar levels as it is high in soluble fibre, helping to slow down the rate of glucose absorption.

FACT

Bees are attracted to the scent of the buckwheat flower and as a result can produce a strongly flavoured dark honey.

Hans Christian Andersen once wrote a story about the pride and vainglory of the Buckwheat plant struck by a lightning in a storm.

Millet

Before the cultivation of rice, millet was a wild grain growing across Africa and Asia. It is quite often compared to corn, as it grows and looks like a grain, if a very little one. It grows fairly rapidly and doesn't need much water, so it's often farmed in dry areas where wheat and barley can't be grown.

The traditional way to harvest millet was through a process of winnowing to loosen the grain from the husks and straw, which, in its simplest form, involves throwing the grain into the air to allow the wind to remove the chaff.

From Africa, where they use millet primarily for porridge, the grain then spread to India, where they use it as a flour to make roti. In Europe it is often used like a polenta, and in Italy a millet porridge known as *puls* was eaten before the introduction of both corn and polenta.

TASTE

These little yellow grains are mild, fairly neutral in flavour and when cooked are of a delicate texture. They become full when boiled whole, or incredibly soft and creamy when cooked from flakes. The grains are often toasted ahead of cooking, giving them a slightly nutty flavour.

A number of countries across the world use millet for porridge. In Senegal they make *fondé* by boiling millet flakes with condensed milk and butter; in Tamil Nadu, India, they make a porridge called *koozh* and regularly sell it as street food; in many parts of the world it is simply cooked like a polenta, served as a savoury dish. After soaking the grain, I like to add it to batters when baking to give an amazing additional texture to both sweet and savoury treats, from Millet, Spinach and Cheddar Muffins to Baked Millet Slices (see pages 88 and 194).

NUTRITION

Millet is easy to digest, rich in amino acids and a gluten-free alternative to other grains. It is a great source of protein and fibre as well as manganese, a mineral that helps improve the health of bones, muscles and nerves. It also contains magnesium to help reduce cholesterol, phosphorus to help the body process carbohydrates, fats and proteins and copper to maintain and improve the metabolism.

FACT

Egyptians would make flat breads out of millet and store them in the same place where beer was produced. A consequence of this was that the yeast from the beer would occasionally contaminate the dough of the bread, resulting in the earliest signs of a raised millet bread.

Oats

ORIGIN

When we think of oats, most of us think of the classic Scottish oat. In fact, the modern oat is historically linked to the wild red oat, a grass that grows widespread in Africa, Australia and Asia and was originally used for medicinal purposes. Today, oats grow best in temperate climates and have a great tolerance to rain, performing best in the northern regions of Europe and Iceland – ideal oat conditions include long summer days, cool temperatures and periods of high rainfall that help the grain to swell naturally and produce a sweet plump golden oat.

TASTE

Compared to other grains, oats are relatively soft. They're high in beta-glucan, a compound that is released when oats are soaked, providing them with their distinct creaminess. These characteristics make them slightly sweet, sometimes smelling almost like maple syrup when they're freshly rolled.

There are a number of different ways in which oats can be harvested for consumption. The whole oat is called a groat, where the outer hull of the grain has been removed, leaving the whole grain intact. Traditionally these haven't been popular to cook with and are more often than not cut, rolled or milled for use. Pinhead oats or steel-cut oats, also known as oatmeal, are oat groats that have been cut and cracked into smaller pieces, available in different grinds; rough, medium and fine. Oatmeal is used to make traditional Scottish porridge, cooked slowly with water and sea salt and stirred clockwise with a thin wooden stirring stick called a spurtle.

The most commonly produced oats are rolled oats or 'flaked' oats. Jumbo rolled oats are produced by simply rolling the whole groat through a flaker, whereas porridge oats are marginally more processed, being cut and then finely rolled. In the shop we like to use oat groats, which we then roll ourselves to create fresh oat flakes (rolled oats) but a combination of jumbo and porridge oats works well to make the perfect bowl of porridge if you can't get hold of oat groats.

More recently, oat flour has been used for baked goods such as biscuits and cakes as well as breads and is thought to have originated in Britain; try my Yogurt Cake with Prune and Fennel Compote (see page 212). Meanwhile, in South America they make a popular sweet drink called avena, which combines ground oats, milk and spices.

NUTRITION

Oats are quite the wonder grain. They're a rich source of fibre, iron and essential minerals such as magnesium and zinc, all of

which aid the healthy functioning of the body. The beta-glucan component of the grain is a type of soluble fibre that monitors how much carbohydrate is absorbed into the blood stream. It actually slows this process down, providing longer, slow releasing energy, thus preventing dramatic spikes in blood sugar levels and insulin and discouraging our bodies from producing and storing too much fat. In addition to this, beta-glucan is said to help the functioning of our immune system, enhancing its ability to navigate and respond to infections and bad bacteria.

Globulin is a protein that is only found in oat grains; it is the same protein you get from eating meat, milk and eggs.

Oats also help to lower cholesterol. They also relax blood vessels, easing pressure around the heart muscle and therefore helping to keep the heart healthy.

Oats are naturally gluten free, but may be contaminated during the growing process if they have been sown in a field that has previously grown a crop that contains wheat. They can also be contaminated during the milling process if they have passed through a machine that has previously rolled a grain that contains gluten.

FACT

Oats have been used regularly to sooth skin conditions and irritations such as eczema, either as a body cream or by sprinkling oats into a bath of warm water.

Oliver Cromwell's drink of choice was said to be one of ale, oatmeal and spices (allspice and cinnamon), known as an oatmeal caudle.

Quinoa

ORIGIN

Quinoa is another pseudograin (see page 27), but is also considered an ancient grain, untouched since it was first cultivated and harvested in the Andes mountains – the Incas referred to it as the 'mother grain'.

Quinoa is a member of the grass family and is closely related to beetroot and spinach. It is hardy and grows in a range of colours from white, black and red.

TASTE

Quinoa grows a natural outer coating called saponin, a bitter layer designed to deter pests. Soaking and rinsing quinoa breaks this down and reduces the bitter taste (see page 48).

Quinoa is light both in texture and taste and so works well with a range of flavours, pairing well with spices and fresh herbs. Whole quinoa works perfectly in salads, or alongside a main dish. I personally use flaked quinoa sparingly as it can taste of the bitter outer layer, so instead of using quinoa flakes for porridge, I use whole quinoa and cook it with a little milk (see page 66). Popped (or puffed) quinoa is super for sprinkling on salads for a little crunch. Puffed quinoa can be found in some specialist stores and it makes a crunchy, light treat. Toasting quinoa before you cook with it makes it slightly nutty and fragrant.

Quinoa is usually cooked in boiling water; red and black quinoa take longer to cook than white and have a much firmer texture.

NUTRITION

Researcher and writer Philip White once said, 'While no single food can supply all the essential life sustaining nutrients, quinoa comes as close as any other in the plant or animal kingdom.' It's certainly true that this grain is considered something of a wonder grain and is often referred to as a superfood. High in protein, nutrients and essential amino acids, as well as being a rich source of iron, magnesium and fibre, this grain is set to keep you feeling in tip-top shape.

FACT

The botanical name for quinoa is Chenopodium and means 'goose foot', so called because the leaves of the plant look like webbed goose feet.

Rice

ORIGIN

Rice is the most popular grain to eat in the world (although more corn than rice is produced, it is mainly used for purposes other than human consumption). It can be sown on a number of different terrains, growing particularly well in areas of high rainfall. The traditional method of flooding rice fields is actually a way of keeping pests at bay, and the fields are then drained before the harvest. Today rice is grown on every continent except Antarctica, resulting in a huge diversity in the way it is cooked, consumed and, indeed, the role it plays within societies.

TASTE

The different varieties of rice are mainly to do with colour – including white, brown, red, black and purple – and size of grain. Long grain rice maintains its texture and shape throughout cooking, making it a perfect side to curries, pilafs and salads. Medium grain rice contains slightly more starch, resulting in a stickier texture that is perfect for risotto and paella. Short grain rice is most commonly found in sweet dishes and works well in puddings and porridges. The range of varieties means that rice is probably the most versatile of all grains – cuisines across the world use it in soups, with fish, poultry or meat, as a stuffing for vegetables or wrapped in seaweed or leaves, as a pudding, in breads and even as a sweet or savoury porridge. I tend to favour brown rice for its nuttier texture, as well as the more unusual red rice and Chinese black sticky rice (see page 98 for my Black Sticky Rice and Coconut Porridge). Rice should be soaked in cold water before cooking (see page 48).

NUTRITION

The nutritional profile of rice depends on the variety and how it has been grown and processed but, as a rule of thumb, brown rice is significantly higher in basic nutrients such as vitamins and minerals as well as fibre, because a lot of this is stored in the husks. As with vegetables, darker-hued colours of rice are thought to have antioxidant properties, with red and black varieties offering even more nutritional benefits.

FACT

In Asia, rice finds its way into everyday language: in Japan the word for 'meal' is the same as the word for 'rice' and in China the literal translation of the question, 'How are you?' is actually 'Have you had your rice today?'

Rye

ORIGIN

Originally thought to be a weed, this golden-green hued grain has long been overlooked. Rye's ability to grow in tough sandy or peaty soils and survive through treacherous cold winters has enabled it to flourish, despite not being formally farmed until fairly recently.

Today, it is grown primarily in Northern Europe. Farming rye benefits the land that it grows on; its deep root structure enables it to capture more nutrients than other grains and improves the health of the soil.

Unfortunately, cultivation of rye has fallen recently as there has been a lack of demand, but this unique tasting grain is not one to overlook. It is commonly used as a flour and made into breads, most famously pumpernickel. Optimistically, a number of European countries are now using rye berries in their cooking and cereals.

TASTE

Rye has a very distinct, rich and earthy taste and works well with spices suited to its origin such as cardamom, cinnamon and caraway seeds. On its own it has a taste like no other grain; it's sometimes associated with sourness, like a levain or starter. It could be considered an acquired taste and hasn't always been to everyone's liking – it was often mixed with spelt to dilute its taste.

The most traditional use for rye is in bread. From the same family as wheat, rye contains gluten (although much less than wheat), making it a good ingredient for bread and crispbreads. I've used it in a number of recipes, including Carrot Rye Pancakes (see page 92) and have also blitzed it to a flour with rolled outs to make a delicate rye pastry (see page 160).

Like barley, rye can be distilled and used for alcoholic drinks, most notably rye whiskeys and beers.

NUTRITION

Rye includes a fibre called arabinoxylan, which is high in antioxidant activity, binding and then drawing the toxins out of your body as you digest it. For the many people who are avoiding overly refined wheat or with only a slight intolerance to gluten, rye is a great alternative, being high in gliadin and low in glutenin. Rye is also a rich source of fibre and has a high content of nutrients such as selenium, phosphorous, magnesium, copper, zinc and protein.

FACT

Although no longer an issue in farming today, rye can become infected with the ergot fungus, which can cause hallucinations. Ergot-infected rye is said to have been to blame for the claims of witchcraft during the Salem Witch Trials in Massachusetts, USA in 1692.

Spelt

ORIGIN

Spelt is an ancient grain thought to have been popular in Ancient Greece; Greek mythology mentions spelt as a gift from Demeter, the goddess of harvest. Spelt is actually a subspecies of wheat but its thick husks are harder to remove and so the grain is not as suitable for mass production. However, these thick husks are a natural way to protect the crop from pollutants and insects, making it a great grain to grow free from chemicals. As a result, spelt has remained un-hybridised or chemically altered, unlike wheat which was put in the service of mass-production.

TASTE

Spelt is available as whole, pearled spelt, spelt flakes and as a flour, making it a versatile grain that is also useful for baking. As a species of wheat, spelt also contains gluten, although in much smaller quantities than the common wheat, making it good for creating an elastic structure in bread and pastries. I use it to make both pitta bread and waffles (see page 90 and 96).

Spelt's flavour is subtle, sometimes likened to a light rye – nutty, earthy and faintly sweet. As for its texture, the grain is pronounced and chewy, similar to barley. The earthy tone makes it perfect for cooking with root vegetables such as beetroot and Jerusalem artichoke. More recently, particularly in Scandinavian countries, pearled spelt has been popular in dishes such as risotto – unlike rice, it doesn't need to be stirred constantly.

To get the best from spelt, the key is the speed with which you use it. Allow a loaf to rise over a long time, soak the grains well and always cook slowly.

NUTRITION

Like a number of whole grains, spelt is a great source of protein, dietary fibre and B vitamins. It is particularly rich in minerals such as manganese and phosphorus, helping slow down the absorption of sugar into the blood and to maintain healthy bones.

As mentioned above, it does contain a moderate amount of gluten, but compared to wheat it is a more soluble protein. Unlike in wheat production, spelt is not overly processed, therefore maintains the vital bran and germ during milling.

FACT

Spelt has been distilled to create a number of different alcohols and spirits: in Holland, it has been used to make a gin called Genever, in Bavaria it has been brewed as a beer and in Poland it is distilled to make vodka.

Soaking Grains

The process of soaking grains is a traditional and an age-old one, helping to break down the naturally occurring tough outer layer of any grain, which is hard to digest. It also makes their nutrients more bioavailable.

The process of harvesting grains means that they are gathered before they flower. Because of this, the grains still have their protective layer of phytic acid, an 'anti-nutrient' that ensures the grain maintains its important minerals in order to form fully. It is also a way for the grains to naturally ward off pests and insects that might eat them and prevent them from spreading. When consumed, this phytic acid, although not harmful, doesn't allow us to completely absorb the health-giving minerals and nutrients from the grain, so blocking the absorption of iron, magnesium, zinc and so on.

Simply soaking your grains, nuts and legumes in water enormously improves their nutritional profiles. To take it even further, adding an acidic medium helps to make the process more effective. It adds a stage of fermentation to the soaking process, making the foods easier to digest. Be warned, this can change the taste of a dish, but not to the point that you should shy away from trying this. It can make the grains slightly sour: delicious in a savoury dish and somewhat refreshing in a sweet one. Acidic mediums can come in the form of both lactose acids (whole milk, kefir, yogurt and buttermilk) and dairy-free acids (apple cider vinegar, lemon juice and coconut kefir). My personal favourite is apple cider vinegar or lemon juice. For best results, mix at least 1 teaspoon of your chosen acidic medium to every 250ml of soaking liquid.

Most of the recipes recommend soaking the grains in cold water for anything from 30 minutes to overnight. If you've forgotten to soak grains that call for an overnight soak, a good trick is to speed up the soaking process by using an acidic medium, chosen from the options above. But do give it a go; it's fun, and adds a satisfyingly different flavour to a simple dish.

After you have soaked your grains, make sure you rinse them well in cold water and drain thoroughly before cooking.

How to Sprout

The best grains to sprout are whole grains, husks included.
It is possible to sprout grains that have been hulled, but not to
the same extent. However, it does still improve the nutritional
composition of the grain. But do try and sprout the whole spelt,
whole barley or whole oat, germ and bran intact.

The first stage of sprouting is soaking or activating the grain.
This breaks down the outer acidic layer of the grain and increases
moisture content. This activation stage allows you to make 'milk'
from the grains, by blending them with 4 parts water.

After soaking the grains, you rinse them under cold water,
drain them, and then place them in a bowl in a cool place. The
grains need to be rinsed every 12 hours, morning and evening.
Depending on the grain and its composition, whether it's a
pseudograin or soft or hard grain, this stage can take between
1–5 days. Some people cover the bowl with a sprouting lid or
screen but you could cover it with cheesecloth or a tea towel and
a rubber band, and then leave it turned upside down at a slight
angle to drain the water. I've done without this step and in a bowl
and it also works – the only risk is that the excess water might
make the grains start to mould. After this you can use the sprouted
grains on salads or dehydrate them and mill them to a flour.

For a jar or small bowl's worth, sprout ½ cup of the grain. Once
sprouted, refrigerate for 4–7 days.

GRAIN	HOURS TO SOAK	DAYS TO SPROUT
Amaranth	8	1–2
Barley	6	2
Buckwheat	6	2–3
Millet	5	12hrs
Oats	6–8	2–3
Quinoa	4	2–3
Rice	9	3–5
Rye	6–8	2
Spelt	6–8	2

BREAKFAST

Hazelnut and Butter Porridge

René Redzepi from famed Copenhagen restaurant Noma once said that nothing beats a good bowl of top quality steaming grains with a pad of butter on top and I'd have to agree. It's an indulgent Scandinavian tradition – once the butter hits the warm porridge, it starts to melt and carries the coconut palm sugar to the edge of the bowl, creating a subtly sweet caramel. This recipe hits the spot every time and is a great way to start the day.

• SERVES 2

FOR THE PORRIDGE
100g rolled oats, soaked in
    250ml water for at least
    30 minutes
250ml unsweetened
    almond milk
¼ teaspoon sea salt

TO SERVE
¼ teaspoon ground cinnamon
1 tablespoon coconut palm sugar
2 slices of salted organic butter
2 tablespoons roasted
    hazelnuts, skins removed,
    finely chopped
½ red apple, coarsely grated
    or finely chopped

• Place the porridge ingredients, including the water the oats have been soaked in, into a pan over a medium heat and cook for 3–4 minutes, stirring continuously, until the oats start to come together.

Prepare the toppings by stirring the ground cinnamon into the coconut palm sugar.

As soon as the porridge is cooked, spoon into 2 bowls and top with the butter, cinnamon coconut palm sugar, hazelnuts and grated apple.

NOTE
If you have any leftover porridge when making this or other porridge recipes, try turning it into a pancake using the method on page 219.

Blackberry, Bay and Cacao Porridge

As sad as it is to see summer fading, it's tempered by the knowledge that there will be gluts of blackberries among the brambles. The secret is to grab as many as you can when they're ripe and figure out what to do with them later; compotes, jams, chutneys, the list is never-ending. This is one of my favourite recipes to welcome in the new season's fruits.

- SERVES 2

FOR THE PORRIDGE
100g rolled oats, soaked
   in 250ml water for
   at least 30 minutes
250ml unsweetened
   almond milk
¼ teaspoon sea salt
1 teaspoon coconut oil
2 teaspoons raw cacao powder

FOR THE BLACKBERRY COMPOTE
250g blackberries
1 tablespoon maple syrup
1 bay leaf
Squeeze of lemon juice

TO SERVE
2 tablespoons blackberry
   compote
½ red apple, coarsely grated
   or finely chopped
2 tablespoons Almond Butter
   from a jar or homemade
   (see page 240)
1 teaspoon bee pollen (optional)

- First make the blackberry compote by placing the blackberries, maple syrup, bay leaf and lemon juice in a small pan with 1 tablespoon of water and allow to come to the boil. Once bubbling, take it off the heat and set aside.

Place all the porridge ingredients, including the water the oats have been soaked in, into a pan over a medium heat and cook for 3–4 minutes, stirring continuously, until the oats start to come together, the coconut oil has melted and the cacao powder has blended in.

Spoon into 2 bowls and top with the blackberry compote, grated apple, almond butter and bee pollen, if using.

Blueberry Porridge

When we opened the shop in June 2015, this blueberry porridge was one of the first on the menu and it was an instant hit. It's a firm favourite when the berry season is underway. There is something so delicious when blueberries and maple come together. The sweet and sour berry and dark treacle syrup paired with creamy, salted oats makes this such a moreish breakfast.

- SERVES 2

FOR THE PORRIDGE
100g rolled oats, soaked
 in 250ml water
 for at least 30 minutes
250ml unsweetened
 almond milk
¼ teaspoon sea salt

FOR THE BLUEBERRY COMPOTE
250g blueberries
1 tablespoon maple syrup
Squeeze of lemon juice

TO SERVE
2 tablespoons mixed seeds,
 such as flaxseeds, pumpkin
 seeds, sunflower seeds
Few strawberries, sliced
2 tablespoons coconut flakes
2 tablespoons Almond Butter
 from a jar or homemade
 (see page 240)
2 tablespoons amaranth
 (optional)

- First make the blueberry compote: place the blueberries, maple syrup and lemon juice into a small pan with 1 tablespoon of water and allow to come to the boil. Once bubbling, take it off the heat and set aside.

Place the porridge ingredients, including the water the oats have been soaked in, into a pan over a medium heat and cook for 3–4 minutes, stirring continuously, until the oats have come together.

Spoon into 2 bowls and add the toppings in this order: a tablespoon of blueberries in a line down the middle with a pool of juice around the edge, then the seeds, strawberry slices, coconut flakes, almond butter and amaranth, if using.

Øllebrød (Rye Porridge)

Rye is a wonderfully rich and unique-tasting grain with its own strong, earthy flavour. It can hold a lot of spice so don't hold back and don't be scared to experiment with spices that you don't normally use. Do you favour cinnamon? How about nutmeg this time? Øllebrød is a traditional Danish porridge that uses leftover stale rye bread – nothing goes to waste. It's filling and delicious and completely different to any porridge I've ever tasted.

• SERVES 2 HUNGRY SOULS

FOR THE PORRIDGE
200g fresh or stale rye bread, crusts removed, torn into pieces
½ teaspoon coconut palm sugar
1 teaspoon ground cinnamon
Seeds from ½ vanilla pod or ½ teaspoon vanilla extract
Finely grated zest of ¼ unwaxed lemon
¼ teaspoon sea salt

FOR THE CARDAMOM MAPLE SYRUP
Seeds from 10 cardamom pods, ground in a pestle and morter
250ml maple syrup

TO SERVE
2 tablespoons roasted hazelnuts, skin removed, finely chopped
1 pear, skinned, cored and sliced
2 tablespoons Greek yogurt

• First make the cardamom maple syrup. Place the ingredients into a small pan with 1 tablespoon of water and bring to the boil. Once bubbling, take it off the heat and leave to infuse while you make the porridge.

Place the porridge ingredients into a pan over a medium heat with 600ml of water, bring to the boil, then reduce the heat and let it bubble away for 15–20 minutes, stirring occasionally, until it has a porridge-like consistency.

Spoon into 2 bowls and top with the hazelnuts, diced pear, yogurt and cardamom maple syrup.

How to build a porridge

You can make porridge with any of the grains featured in this book, whether whole or flaked. Simply choose your grain and follow one of the methods below, using the table opposite to work out the ratio of grain to water. Customise your porridge by adding your choice of LIQUID, CREAM, SPICE or CRUNCH – the variations are endless.   All the quantities given are to serve 2, but can easily be halved or multiplied.

WHOLE

Fully submerge the grains in water and soak for at least 1 hour, preferably 6. This activates the grains and breaks down their naturally occurring acidic layer, allowing us to digest them more easily.   Drain the grains and cook them over a medium heat in the appropriate amount of water (see opposite). Once this has been absorbed, add your LIQUID of choice and continue cooking – whole grains take about 20 minutes to become porridge-like. Add a little more liquid if needed until the porridge comes together the way you like it.   Season with a good pinch of sea salt and/or your chosen SPICE.
  Top with one of the CREAM options and sprinkle over some CRUNCH before serving.

FLAKED

Soak 1 cup flaked grains in 1 cup of water for at least 1 hour, preferably 6. This activates them and breaks down their naturally occurring acidic layer, allowing us to digest them more easily.   Add the grains and the water they've been soaked in to a pan. Add 1 cup of LIQUID of your choice and start to cook over a medium heat for 3–4 minutes.
  As the porridge starts to come together add a good pinch of salt and/or your chosen SPICE.   Top with one of the CREAM options and sprinkle over some CRUNCH before serving.

LIQUID

Whole milk
Coconut milk
Almond milk
Oat milk
Hazelnut milk
Seed milk
Hemp milk
Sesame milk
Apple juice
Carrot juice
Ginger juice
Stock

SPICE

(¼–½ teaspoon
  per serving)
Ground cinnamon
Ground cardamom
Ground/grated ginger
Vanilla seeds
Ground turmeric
Black pepper
Ground nutmeg
Ground cloves
Ground cumin
Ground fennel
Chilli powder
Ground coriander
Caraway seeds
  (crushed)

GRAIN AND CHARACTER	WHOLE GRAIN TO LIQUID
AMARANTH Fine, light, every so slightly nutty	1 cup to 2 cups water + 2 cups liquid of choice
BARLEY Textured, a lot of bite, versatile and great with strong flavours	½ cup to 3 cups water + 1 cup liquid of choice
QUINOA Mild, great with spices and fresh flavours, quite a fine grain	1 cup to 2 cups water + 1 cup liquid of choice
OATS Creamy, slightly sweet	1 cup to 1 cup water + 1 cup liquid of choice
BUCKWHEAT Strongly flavoured, relatively soft in texture	1 cup to 2 cups water + 1 cup liquid of choice
RICE: **SHORT GRAIN BROWN RICE** **AND CHINESE BLACK STICKY RICE** Glutinous, naturally sweet	½ cup to 2 cups water + 1 cup liquid of choice
SPELT Nutty, grows plump both whole and flaked	½ cup to 2 cups water + 1 cup liquid of your choice
RYE Yeasty flavour, can hold a lot of spice	½ cup to 2 cups water + 1 cup liquid of choice
MILLET Mild in flavour, similar to rice, unique texture	1 cup to 2 cups water + 1 cup liquid of choice

CREAM

Butter
Yogurt
Coconut yogurt
Skyr
Nut butter
Tahini
Sour cream
Crème fraîche

CRUNCH

Seeds
Almonds
Hazelnuts
Pecans
Cacao nibs
Granola
Coconut flakes

Barley Porridge with Salted Pear Compote and Pistachio Sesame Sprinkle

I have a pear tree in my garden, in the middle of Hackney. It makes the summer so much better; when it swells with fruit, it takes everything in me to be patient and let them ripen. When they're just about to drop I pick as many as I can carry and cook them with maple syrup and coconut oil for a light caramel. I like adding soaked, rinsed barley to this porridge because it lends a chewy, slightly fermented taste that pairs particularly well with the sweet fruit.

- SERVES 2

FOR THE PORRIDGE
50g barley flakes mixed
   with 50g rolled oats,
   soaked in 250ml water
   for at least 30 minutes
100ml coconut milk
½ teaspoon sea salt
½ teaspoon vanilla extract

FOR THE SALTED PEAR COMPOTE
2 pears, cored and diced or
   sliced (or however you like)
1 tablespoon coconut oil
1 tablespoon maple syrup
¼–½ teaspoon sea salt
   (depending on how salty you
   like it)

TO SERVE
2 tablespoons Greek yogurt
½ teaspoon ground cinnamon
1 tablespoon finely
   chopped pistachios
1 tablespoon sesame seeds

- Make the salted pear compote first: combine the pear, coconut oil, maple syrup and salt in a pan and place over a medium heat. Bring to the boil, then turn down the heat and simmer for 8–10 minutes until the pear is just tender and the caramel is thickening.

Place the porridge ingredients, 150ml of water and the liquid the grains have been soaked in into a pan over a medium heat and cook for 4–5 minutes, stirring continuously, until it all comes together (the barley may take a little longer to cook than normal oat porridge).

Prepare the toppings by mixing the yogurt and cinnamon together and separately mixing the pistachios and sesame seeds.

Spoon into 2 bowls and top with the salted pear compote, cinnamon yogurt and pistachio sesame sprinkle.

Rhubarb and Buckwheat Porridge with Cardamom Granola

This porridge makes me happy. It's nostalgic and sweet and a welcome pink pop in the middle of winter. When buying rhubarb, make sure the ends snap easily and some sap comes out. Like brothers with different hair colours, rhubarb and buckwheat are from the same family of flowering plants, known as Polygonaceae, so they meld harmoniously.

- SERVES 2

FOR THE PORRIDGE
100g buckwheat groats,
   thoroughly rinsed, soaked
   in 250ml water for at least
   1 hour
250ml Oat Milk (see page 234)
¼ teaspoon sea salt

FOR THE RHUBARB COMPOTE
350g rhubarb, washed,
   trimmed and chopped
   into 3cm pieces
30g coconut palm sugar
Finely grated zest and juice
   of ½ unwaxed orange
½ teaspoon root ginger, peeled
   and chopped (optional)

TO SERVE
2 tablespoons Cardamom
   Granola (see page 72)
2 tablespoons skyr
   or Greek yogurt
2 teaspoons toasted
   coconut flakes

- Preheat the oven to 180°C/fan 160°C/350°F/gas mark 4. Prepare the rhubarb compote by mixing the rhubarb, coconut palm sugar, orange zest and juice and ginger, if using, in a mixing bowl until the rhubarb is nicely coated. Tip into a small roasting tray, add about 4 tablespoons of water and bake for 20–30 minutes until the rhubarb is completely soft.

Meanwhile, make the porridge by placing all the ingredients, including the water the grains have been soaked in, into a pan and place over a medium heat. Cook for 20 minutes, stirring continuously, until it all comes together.

Spoon the porridge into 2 bowls and top with the rhubarb compote, granola and skyr or Greek yogurt.

Rugbrød Granola

I could create a whole book with recipes for leftover rye. I love rye – especially rye bread – so much so that it breaks my heart to see any part of it thrown away. Fresh bread doesn't last long and being such a labour of love to make, it's nice to have a handful of recipes to make sure you aren't wasting any part of it. Granolas, stuffing and croutons are just a few ways to keep enjoying it for days on end. Try this for a filling and delicious way to enjoy rye bread and give granola a new taste and texture.

- SERVES 2

200g stale rye bread, crusts removed, torn into very small pieces
2 tablespoons coconut oil, melted
35g coconut palm sugar
1 teaspoon ground cinnamon
50g almonds, finely chopped

- Preheat the oven to 160°C/fan 140°C/325°F/gas mark 3 and line a baking tray with baking paper.

Place all the ingredients into a mixing bowl and mix well with your hands so everything is nicely coated.

Spread out on the baking tray, pop in the oven and bake for 20 minutes, checking it and giving it a stir after 10 minutes. Leave to cool before serving with your choice of yogurt or milk.

NOTE
Almonds that have been activated have a much more satisfying and clean crunch once roasted; it also increases the nutrient value of the nuts and makes them easier to digest. To activate the almonds, soak overnight in water, drain and then set aside until completely dry. Once they're dry, crush or finely chop them and bake with the rest of the granola.

Cinnamon and Banana
Quinoa Porridge

I tend to keep this a little runnier than a normal porridge, as quinoa has a great texture and can be very filling. It's good to keep the consistency quite light and not stir too much, which will make this gummy. This recipe works well particularly with leftover quinoa (I find that making too much quinoa is a common occurrence) but remember to leave out the salt if you seasoned the quinoa when you cooked it the first time.

• SERVES 2

FOR THE PORRIDGE
100g whole quinoa, rinsed
    well and soaked in water
    for at least 30 minutes
250ml unsweetened
    almond milk
1 teaspoon ground cinnamon
½ teaspoon sea salt

TO SERVE
1 banana, sliced
2 tablespoons coconut yogurt
1 tablespoon Almond Butter
    from a jar or homemade
    (see page 240)
1 tablespoon cacao nibs
1 tablespoon date syrup
    (or honey)

• Drain and rinse the soaked quinoa well and place in a small pan. Pour over 250ml of water, bring to the boil and cook for 15 minutes until tender and the water has all been absorbed.

Pour in the almond milk, cinnamon and salt and simmer over a medium heat for 7 minutes, stirring continuously, until it has a porridge-like consistency.

Spoon into 2 bowls and top with sliced banana, coconut yogurt, almond butter, cacao nibs and date syrup.

Ginger and Peach Bircher Muesli Pots

• SERVES 4

200g rolled oats
4 tablespoons chia seeds
800ml unsweetened
  almond milk
Juice and finely grated zest
  of ½ unwaxed lemon
2 peaches, pitted and sliced
2 tablespoons honey
1 teaspoon grated root ginger
4 teaspoons chopped pistachios

For this recipe you can either use fresh peaches if they're lovely and ripe, or grill them for 20 minutes until they're smoky and caramelised. This recipe is cool and creamy – perfect for a summer's breakfast. It is also incredibly versatile: try adding different spices such as turmeric, cinnamon or cacao nibs to the grains as they soak. The compote is flexible too, and can work well with any fruit that's in season, such as strawberries or blueberries in summer or persimmons in autumn.

• Mix the oats and chia seeds together before adding the almond milk and a squeeze of the lemon juice. Leave in the fridge to soak for 2–3 hours (or overnight if you're making this for breakfast).

Place the peaches, honey, ginger, lemon zest and remaining juice in a blender and whizz to a purée.

Divide the purée between four glass ramekins and then spoon equal portions of the soaked bircher muesli on top. Serve immediately or chill and serve the next day.

Miso Rice Porridge
with Mango and Hazelnuts

When the excitement of having secured the Neal's Yard site subsided and the reality of what lay ahead set in, I had to get a move on with filling the space. My aunt Melita came to the rescue, inviting me to the Ardingly Antiques Fair for a long day of scouring for furniture. It was a crisp spring morning and this dish warmed us up perfectly without being heavy. The sweet miso is so unique and salty, pairing perfectly with the fresh mango and coconut.

- **SERVES 2**

FOR THE PORRIDGE

100g short grain brown rice, soaked in water for at least 30 minutes
1 tablespoon organic sweet white miso paste
1 tablespoon honey
½ teaspoon coconut oil

TO SERVE

1 mango, peeled, stoned and sliced
2 tablespoons roasted hazelnuts, skins removed, finely chopped
1 tablespoon coconut yogurt
1 tablespoon toasted coconut flakes
1 tablespoon cacao nibs

- Drain and rinse the soaked brown rice then transfer to a medium pan and cover with 650ml water. Add the white miso paste, honey and coconut oil and place over a medium heat.

Bring to the boil, then reduce the heat a little and cook for 40–50 minutes until the rice has softened and has a porridge-like consistency, adding more water if needed.

Remove from the heat and set aside while you prepare your toppings.

Spoon into 2 bowls and top with the mango, hazelnuts, coconut yogurt, coconut flakes and cacao nibs.

Cardamom Granola

- MAKES 800G
  (16 SERVINGS)

300g rolled oats
100g mixed seeds, such as
    pumpkin seeds, sunflower
    seeds, linseeds
100g mixed nuts, such as
    almonds, hazelnuts, walnuts,
    finely chopped
125ml olive oil or coconut oil
125ml maple syrup
1 tablespoon ground cinnamon
Seeds from 4 cardamom pods,
    ground in a mortar and pestle
50g toasted coconut flakes

Granola is one of my favourite things to bake. You can throw in almost any spice, grain, popped grain, seed or nut and you'll make something delicious each time. The key to success is to use top-quality spices, oil (olive or coconut) and sweetener (maple syrup). This is a fail-safe granola recipe that I make daily at the shop.

Play with different types, or a mix of grains depending on what you're in the mood for. Buckwheat groats will give you earthiness, quinoa flakes will give you a rich, crisp texture and puffed millet will give you a pop. You can't really go wrong mixing and matching flavours either: chuck in some orange zest, cacao nibs, even grated carrot and discover your favourite combo.

- Preheat the oven to 160°C/fan 140°C/325°F/gas mark 3 and line a baking tray with baking paper.

Place all the ingredients except the coconut flakes into a mixing bowl and mix well with your hands so everything is nicely coated.

Spread out on the baking tray, then pop into the oven to bake for 40 minutes, stirring every 10 minutes, until it has turned a lovely golden colour. Remove from the oven and, and while still warm, stir in the coconut flakes.

Leave to cool before serving with your choice of yogurt or milk.

Basic Muesli Mix

This is such a handy mix to have in your repertoire. If you're in a rush in the morning or need a pick-me-up in the afternoon, this muesli has the perfect blend of grains, nuts, seeds, fruits and spices. Enjoy with your preferred milk or yogurt, or you can even use it as a base for your porridge. Feel free to add any superfoods or powders that you might like – hemp seeds and maca powder are slightly sweet and work really well.

• MAKES 8 SERVINGS

3 tablespoons coconut flakes
100g rolled oats
100g rye flakes
100g barley flakes
35g popped buckwheat
35g popped quinoa
3 tablespoons goji berries
3 tablespoons dried berries
   (raisins, cranberries,
   blueberries)
6 tablespoons nuts (such as
   brazil, hazelnut, almond,
   macadamia)
3 tablespoons chia seeds
3 tablespoons sesame seeds
2 teaspoons spice (ground
   cinnamon, crushed fennel
   or caraway seeds, or a blend
   of all three)

• Preheat the oven to 170°C/fan 150°C/340°F/gas mark 3½. Place the coconut flakes on a baking tray and bake in the oven for 4–6 minutes, or until the coconut flakes start to golden at the edges, watching carefully so they don't burn as they can turn quickly.

Find a large Tupperware container or lidded jar to mix your muesli in – you'll need something with about a 2-litre capacity.

Mix all the ingredients together in a large bowl, adding your chosen spice at the end. Make sure all the different ingredients are evenly distributed and then transfer to your container or jar.

Savoury Kale Porridge
with Fried Eggs

2 tablespoons olive oil
¼ onion, finely chopped
½ garlic clove, crushed
50g kale, stems discarded,
    torn into small pieces
100g rolled oats (unsoaked)
250ml vegetable stock
Sea salt and black pepper
2 eggs
Small handful of chives
Hot sauce, such as sriracha,
    to serve (optional)

It wasn't until I took part in the World Porridge Championship in Scotland that I became familiar with the concept of savoury porridge. Did I mention that I participated in the World Porridge Championship?! It was Neal Robertson's porridge with pancetta and Parmesan that clinched the idea of savoury porridge for me. Here the naturally sweet oats, cooked with stock and mixed with kale, onion and black pepper is perfect any time of day. Add crispy bacon and roasted mushrooms to make it really decadent.

• Add 1 tablespoon of the oil to a small pan and warm over a medium heat before adding the onion. Cook for 5–7 minutes until soft and sweet. Add the garlic and cook for a minute longer.

Meanwhile, boil the kettle. Place the kale in a large bowl and pour over the boiling water. Let the kale soften and wilt for 2 minutes, making sure the leaves are fully submerged. When the leaves have become a dark rich green, drain the kale and set aside. (Try straining the kale water into a glass and adding a pinch of salt and pepper for a delicious, savoury hot drink.)

Place the rolled oats, stock, 250ml of water, a good pinch of sea salt, the kale, onions and garlic into a pan and cook over a medium heat for 4 minutes, until slightly firmer than the texture of porridge.

Heat the remaining oil in a frying pan over a medium heat and crack in the eggs. Cover with a lid and cook for 3–4 minutes. Spoon the porridge into 2 bowls or plates, then top each with a fried egg, some chopped chives and a pinch of salt and fresh black pepper. Serve with hot sauce, if using.

Cheese, Mustard, Ale and Onion Rye Porridge

Rye and ale are delicious ingredients on their own but together, they're a powerhouse. Each one brings out different aspects of the other, making for a rich kick of flavour. You can keep layering this with strong flavours and it just keeps getting better: extra sharp cheese, Dijon mustard and onions will fire it up. Not to mention if you serve it with a Bloody Mary...

- SERVES 2

FOR THE PORRIDGE
100g rye flakes
250ml ale
250ml vegetable stock
Sea salt and black pepper
100g strong hard cheese,
    such as Gruyère or mature
    Cheddar, sliced

TO SERVE
¼ red onion, very thinly sliced
    and soaked in boiling water
    for 10 minutes
2 poached, boiled or
    fried eggs (optional, but
    highly recommended)
2 teaspoons Dijon mustard
    (optional)

- Place the rye, ale, stock and a good pinch of salt and pepper in a pan and cook over a medium heat until you have a firm consistency, about 6 minutes. Meanwhile preheat the grill to high.

Divide the porridge between 2 ramekins and top each with the sliced cheese. Pop under the grill for a few minutes until the cheese has melted and is starting to turn golden.

Serve each ramekin with a few slices of onion and perhaps a poached, boiled or fried egg, along with a dollop of mustard.

Quinoa, Smoked Salmon, Asparagus and Poached Eggs with Garlic Yogurt

Served with smoked salmon, lemon and dill, this quinoa dish is incredibly refreshing and can be used for a casual breakfast or smart celebration. Soaking the quinoa activates the grain so is always best to do, if you have time. Be sure not to rush the poached eggs, remembering that a gentle boil and a slow whirlpool works every time.

• SERVES 2

100g whole quinoa, rinsed
  and soaked in water
  for at least 30 minutes
Sea salt and black pepper
200g asparagus, tough ends
  snapped off
1 tablespoon olive oil, plus
  a little extra to drizzle
2 eggs, at room temperature
1 tablespoon white wine vinegar
100g smoked salmon
2 lemon wedges
Few sprigs of dill

FOR THE GARLIC YOGURT
250g Greek-style yogurt
1 garlic clove, crushed with
  a little salt
Juice of ½ lemon
1 tablespoon olive oil
Sea salt and black pepper

• Drain and rinse the soaked quinoa and place in a pan with 250ml of water. Bring to the boil, then lower the heat to a simmer and cook for 15–20 minutes until all the water has disappeared. Season, then leave to cool.

While the quinoa is cooking, make the garlic yogurt by mixing together all the ingredients in a small bowl. Season, then set aside.

Bring a pan of water to the boil, place a steamer on top and gently steam (or boil) the asparagus for 3 minutes. Drain and season with a little olive oil, salt and pepper.

Poach the eggs by bringing a small pan of water to a gentle simmer. Add a good pinch of salt and the white wine vinegar. Stir the water once or twice to form a slow whirlpool and drop an egg into the centre of it. Poach for 3 minutes until you can see that the whites are firm. Repeat for the other egg.

Build the dish by piling the quinoa onto 2 plates, drizzle over some olive oil and top with the asparagus, smoked salmon and poached eggs. Add a dollop of garlic yogurt, a wedge of lemon and a good sprig of dill and serve.

Smoothies

There are few smoothies that I would choose in place of breakfast. But here are the ones I'd be happy to regularly indulge in. I need my smoothie to be delicious and fresh, but more importantly not a sugary overload. And I don't want to still feel hungry after drinking them, which is why they're so good with grains mixed in. The grains also make them a lot creamier, which can never be a bad thing. These recipes will keep you full and satisfied right through until lunch. Maca powder and bee pollen are just two of the 'superfood' extras you can add to these smoothies.

BERRY SMOOTHIE

- SERVES 1

25g buckwheat groats,
  soaked in water for
  at least 30 minutes
1 ripe banana
65ml coconut milk
3 tablespoon mixed berries
  (raspberries, strawberries,
  blackberries, blueberries)
Finely grated zest and juice
  of ¼ unwaxed lemon
⅛ teaspoon vanilla extract
4 ice cubes
Fresh or frozen berries,
  to serve

- Rinse the buckwheat groats well under fresh water, then drain and add to a blender with all the remaining ingredients and 65ml of water. Blitz until smooth.

Serve topped with a small handful of fresh or frozen berries.

GREEN SMOOTHIE

- SERVES 1

25g quinoa flakes,
  soaked in water for
  at least 30 minutes
Handful of spinach leaves
¼ avocado
¼ cucumber
125ml apple juice or iced/
  cooled green tea
Small handful of fresh
  mint leaves
Pinch of ground ginger
Pinch of finely grated
  unwaxed lemon zest
4 ice cubes

- Rinse the quinoa flakes under fresh water, then drain and add to a blender with all the remaining ingredients and 65ml of water. Blitz until smooth.

BANANA, TAHINI, CINNAMON AND MACA OAT SMOOTHIE

- SERVES 1

25g rolled oats,
  soaked in water for
  at least 30 minutess
1 ripe banana
125ml unsweetened
  almond milk
1 tablespoon tahini
¼ teaspoon ground cinnamon
½ teaspoon maca powder
  (optional)
4 ice cubes
1 teaspoon bee pollen
  (optional), to serve

- Rinse the rolled oats under fresh water, then drain and add to a blender with all the remaining ingredients, except the bee pollen. Blitz until smooth.

Top with a little bee pollen, if using, and serve.

Rugbrød (Rye Bread)

Rye is a key staple in every Danish larder. Served with salad or as part of a smørrebrød (see page 132), its ubiquitous presence is always welcome. Rye flour itself is enormously flexible and can add a nice malty touch to savoury baking or some sharpness to your sweet. This is an easy and forgiving loaf to make. Just remember to leave it to cool completely before slicing to prevent it crumbling apart.

• MAKES 1 LOAF

10g dried yeast
2 tablespoons honey
500g dark rye flour,
   plus extra for dusting
400g spelt flour
2 teaspoons sea salt
Olive oil, to grease

• Activate the yeast by placing in a bowl and stirring in 50ml of lukewarm water. Leave it to froth for 15 minutes.

Dissolve the honey in 550ml lukewarm water. Put both the flours into a large mixing bowl with the salt and mix well. Make a well in the middle and pour in the frothy yeast, followed by the honey water. Mix the ingredients to form a sticky dough, then tip out onto a floured board or work surface.

Pull and stretch the dough for 5 minutes until it begins to feel elastic. Transfer to a clean, oiled bowl, cover with cling film or a tea towel and place somewhere warm for about 1 hour, or until the dough has risen by half.

Grease a 900g loaf tin with olive oil and dust with flour. Remove the dough from the bowl, place on a lightly floured board and knead again for a minute or two, then transfer to the prepared baking tin. Cover again and return to your warm place for another hour.

Meanwhile preheat the oven to 220°C/fan 200°C/425°F/gas mark 7. Place the bread on the middle shelf and bake for 35–40 minutes, or until crisp and golden on top. Remove from the tin and return to the oven, placing it directly on the oven shelf this time, for another 5 minutes. Remove from the oven and leave to cool completely on a wire rack before slicing.

NOTE
You can also use leftover rye bread to make porridge. See page 58 for the recipe.

Buckwheat Banana Bread

The smell through the house as you bake this delicious and simple banana bread will make your neighbours jealous and it's something I make when I'm craving down-time. It's not too sweet and, with the earthiness of buckwheat, it can be eaten for breakfast, lunch or as a snack with a good pad of butter and some salt. It will last up to five days – provided you don't gobble it all up before then. The riper the bananas, the better for this; when they're soft and starting to turn brown they are at their sweetest. If you see a banana turning and you're not quite ready to bake, the secret is to pop it into the freezer for when you are.

- SERVES 8–10

4 tablespoons coconut oil,
  plus extra to grease
100g buckwheat flakes, blitzed
  to a flour in a food processor
  (or use buckwheat flour)
100g ground almonds
½ teaspoon baking powder
1 teaspoon ground cinnamon
1 teaspoon sea salt
50g walnuts, finely chopped
4 ripe bananas, peeled and
  smooshed
Finely grated zest of
  ½ unwaxed orange
Seeds from ½ vanilla pod
  or ½ teaspoon vanilla extract
4 tablespoons honey
4 medium eggs, beaten

- Preheat the oven to 180°C/fan 160°C/350°F/gas mark 4. Grease a 900g loaf tin and line it with baking paper.

Mix together the buckwheat, almonds, baking powder, cinnamon, salt and walnuts in a large mixing bowl and then fold in the banana, orange zest and vanilla.

Place the coconut oil and honey in a small pan and melt over a low heat. Let the mix cool for a moment, and then fold into the ingredients in the bowl. Stir in the eggs, a little at a time. Pour into the prepared tin and bake for 45–50 minutes, or until golden and a skewer inserted into the middle comes out clean. Leave to cool in the tin for a few minutes before turning out onto a wire rack.

Chai Butternut Squash Muffins

I can't resist the warming blend of chai, particularly in the cooler winter months. These rusty-coloured muffins use the classic chai flavours of cardamom, cinnamon and cloves and are delicious both first thing in the morning with a fresh pot of tea and served as a treat in the afternoon with soft cheese whipped with orange and honey. Butternut squash adds freshness to the muffins and works wonderfully with the creamy oats. I particularly like making these in the autumn, just as the air starts to cool.

- MAKES 24

75ml olive oil, plus extra
    to grease
200g butternut squash, peeled,
    deseeded and cut into cubes
10 large fresh medjool dates,
    pitted
2 medium eggs
100ml unsweetened almond milk
½ teaspoon vanilla extract
100g rolled oats
100g ground almonds
½ teaspoon bicarbonate of soda
1½ teaspoons baking powder
½ teaspoon sea salt
Seeds from 10 cardamom pods,
    ground in a mortar and pestle
¼ teaspoon ground cinnamon
⅛ teaspoon ground cloves
Pinch of black pepper

FOR THE TOPPING (OPTIONAL)
2 tablespoons soft cheese
1 teaspoon honey
Finely grated zest of
    ¼ unwaxed orange

- Preheat the oven to 200°C/fan 180°C/400°F/gas mark 6. Line a 12-hole muffin tray with paper muffin cases or squares of baking paper: simply cut 10cm squares of baking paper, grease the muffin tray holes with a little oil and press into them with a round object such as a tall glass so the paper sticks.

Place the cubed squash and dates into a food processor or blender and whizz together until you have a smooth paste. Add the eggs, oil, almond milk and vanilla and whizz again. Transfer to a mixing bowl, then stir in the remaining dry ingredients, mixing until everything is nicely incorporated.

Fill each hole of the muffin tray with 3 tablespoons of the mixture, then pop into the oven and bake for 25 minutes until golden and an inserted skewer comes out clean. Transfer the muffins to a wire rack to cool and then prepare the tin again, fill with the remaining mixture and bake to make a second batch.

To make the topping, if using, beat together the soft cheese, honey and orange zest until well combined. Spread over the cooled muffins.

Millet, Spinach and Cheddar Muffins

Millet adds a satisfying crunch to this savoury muffin. It's hard to avoid sweet baked goods when you're trying to grab something on the go, but these muffins are a delicious savoury alternative to get your day off to the right start. They work well as midday snacks, too. If you have a madeleine mould you could make mini versions and serve them as canapés – just reduce the baking time to 15–20 minutes.

• MAKES 12

100g rolled oats, blitzed
   to a coarse flour
   in a food processor
100g spelt flour
100g whole millet
1½ teaspoons baking powder
½ teaspoon bicarbonate of soda
1 teaspoon sea salt
2 medium eggs, beaten
2 tablespoons coconut oil,
   melted, plus extra to grease
250ml Oat Milk (see page 234)
100g grated Cheddar,
   plus extra to top
100g spinach, washed and
   finely chopped
Piccalilli, chutney or mustard
   to serve (optional)

• Preheat the oven to 200°C/fan 180°C/400°F/gas mark 6 and prepare a 12-hole muffin tray with paper muffin cases or squares of baking paper (see page 86).

In a large bowl, combine the blitzed rolled oats, spelt and millet together with the baking powder, bicarbonate of soda and salt. In a separate bowl, combine the eggs, coconut oil, oat milk, Cheddar and spinach and mix evenly together.

Stir the wet ingredients into the dry ingredients until fully combined, then fill each hole of the muffin tray with 3 tablespoons of the mixture and top with a little extra Cheddar. Bake for 25 minutes or until an inserted skewer comes out clean. Transfer to a wire rack to cool before serving with a good helping of piccalilli or chutney, if desired.

Spelt and Rosemary Pittas with Apricot Compote and Tahini Yogurt

Rosemary and apricot are a match made in heaven. It is such a joy to cook with herbs that are usually used in savoury dishes and pair them with less traditional ingredients. Pitta bread is surprisingly easy to make and bakes in no time. I tend to cook these in late summer, when apricots are in their prime. Cook the compote until the apricots just start to become soft, but aren't falling apart. Take a bite and get ready for the ooze.

• MAKES 6

FOR THE PITTA
200g spelt flour, plus extra
  for dusting
2 sprigs of rosemary, leaves
  picked and chopped
½ tablespoon sea salt
1 tablespoon fast-action yeast
1 tablespoon olive oil

FOR THE APRICOT COMPOTE
600g apricots, halved and pitted
Seeds from 8 cardamom pods,
  ground in a mortar and pestle
5 tablespoons honey

FOR THE TAHINI YOGURT
2 tablespoons tahini
2 tablespoons honey
400g Greek yogurt

• Prepare the dough first. Put the flour, rosemary and salt into a large mixing bowl and stir with a wooden spoon. Stir in the yeast and make a well in the centre. Pour the olive oil and about 100ml of lukewarm water into the well and combine the ingredients until the dough comes together and stops sticking to the side of the bowl. Tip the dough onto a lightly floured work surface and knead for a good 7–10 minutes until smooth and elastic. Shape into a ball, then place in a clean bowl, cover with a tea towel and place somewhere warm for about 1 hour, or until risen to twice its size.

Meanwhile, prepare the apricot compote. Place all the ingredients in a large pan with 50ml of water and bring to the boil before reducing the heat to a simmer and cooking until the apricots are just falling apart: 10–12 minutes.

Preheat the oven to 220°C/fan 200°C/425°F/gas mark 7 and place a baking tray inside to heat up.

Tip the dough onto a clean work surface lightly dusted with flour, and divide into six even pieces. Roll into oval shapes about ½–1cm thick. Pop the pitta on the (now hot) baking tray and return to the oven to bake for 8–10 minutes, turning them over after 5 minutes, until they balloon and ever-so-slightly crisp up and begin to turn golden.

Meanwhile, make the tahini yogurt. Beat together the tahini and honey until you have a thick paste, then stir into the yogurt.

Pull the pittas from the oven, cut in half and serve immediately with a dollop of the tahini yogurt and a dollop of apricot compote.

Carrot Rye Pancakes

Carrots are naturally very sweet, which is why I love using them in porridges and cakes. I adapted this recipe from a carrot juice porridge recipe that I make at the shop. I added ginger and cinnamon and it was such a punchy combo that I was itching for more ways to whip it up. And the answer is pancakes. (When in doubt, make pancakes.) Combined with creamy oats and earthy rye, this a real winner. And don't forget to add a healthy dousing of fiery ginger maple syrup.

• SERVES 2

FOR THE PANCAKES
100g rye flakes
50g rolled oats
250ml carrot juice
1 banana, roughly chopped
1 carrot, grated
4 medium eggs
1 teaspoon baking powder
¼ teaspoon vanilla extract
½ teaspoon ground cinnamon
½ teaspoon sea salt
2 tablespoons mixed seeds,
   such as flaxseeds, sunflower
   seeds, pumpkin seeds, plus
   extra to serve
Coconut oil or unsalted butter,
   for frying

FOR THE GINGER MAPLE SYRUP
1 tablespoon finely chopped
   root ginger
300ml maple syrup

TO SERVE
Raisins
1 apple, coarsely grated
   or julienned
Coconut yogurt (optional)

• Make the ginger maple syrup first. Place the ginger, maple syrup and 1 tablespoon of water in a small pan and bring to the boil. Remove from the heat and leave to cool and for the flavours to infuse.

Blend all the pancake ingredients except the mixed seeds and coconut oil together in a food processor. Once it comes together as a smooth batter, stir through the mixed seeds.

Melt 1 teaspoon of coconut oil or butter in a large non-stick frying pan over a medium heat; when it's melted and hot, dollop 2–3 tablespoons of the mixture into the pan per pancake, making sure they don't touch. Cook until the edges start to turn golden and bubbles appear on the surface.

Flip the pancakes over and cook the other side for 2–3 minutes until golden and cooked through. Keep the cooked pancakes in a warm oven while you cook the rest.

To serve, pile up a stack of 3–5 pancakes and top with the additional seeds, raisins, apple, coconut yogurt and drizzle of the ginger maple syrup.

Banana, Buckwheat and Millet Waffles

I love the way the maple syrup pools in waffle grooves. I'll be the first to admit that's 90 per cent of the reason why I eat waffles. But adding buckwheat and millet gives you a reason to eat them without syrup – if you felt so inclined – as the double dose of grains adds a lovely crunch. This is a particularly fun dish to make for breakfast with friends. Serve on a large dish with a few forks so everyone can just tuck in.

You'll need a waffle maker to make these (I thoroughly recommend investing in one), although you can use the batter to make regular pancakes instead (see pages 140–141).

- SERVES 2

100g buckwheat groats,
   soaked in cold water with
   1 tablespoon cider vinegar
   for 1 hour (see page 48)
1 large ripe banana,
   roughly chopped
Pinch of sea salt
Seeds from ½ vanilla pod or
   ½ teaspoon vanilla extract
1 tablespoon honey
Finely grated zest of
   ½ unwaxed orange
100g whole millet, soaked
   in cold water for 1 hour
Olive oil, for frying
Butter and maple syrup,
   to serve

- Drain and rinse the buckwheat groats and then add to a food processor with 250ml of water, the banana, salt, vanilla, honey and orange zest and whizz until smooth. Add the drained millet and blend for a few seconds longer. You want the millet to stay more or less intact to give the waffle some texture.

Heat a little coconut oil in a waffle maker and add about 8 tablespoons of the batter. Cook until golden, about 6–8 minutes.

Keep warm while you repeat with the remaining mixture, then stack on a large plate and serve with butter and maple syrup.

Spelt and Parsley Waffles
with Chilli Beans

I love a hearty, savoury option for breakfast. Particularly in the winter. The homemade chilli beans have a lovely, light smokiness to them – cooking them slowly over a low heat adds a great depth of flavour. Adding spinach and parsley to the waffles gives a fresh lightness that pairs well with the earthy spelt. If you'd like to bulk this out further, slice a few portobello mushrooms and cook in a little olive oil, garlic and lemon. If you don't have a waffle maker, you can make these into savoury pancakes (see pages 140–141).

- MAKES 12

FOR THE CHILLI BEANS
1 tablespoon olive oil
1 small onion, thinly sliced
2 garlic cloves, finely chopped
2 red chillies, sliced (deseed
 if you prefer less heat)
1 teaspoon smoked paprika
400g can of chopped tomatoes
1 teaspoon honey
1 tablespoon balsamic vinegar
2 × 400g cans of cannellini beans,
 drained and rinsed
Sea salt and black pepper

FOR THE PANCAKES
250g spelt flakes or spelt flour
1 teaspoon baking powder
3 medium eggs, beaten
350ml coconut milk, buttermilk
 or Oat Milk (see page 234)
1 tablespoon olive or coconut oil,
 plus extra for frying
150g spinach
Small bunch of parsley, leaves
 picked and finely chopped
Finely chopped herbs such
 as chives, to serve

- Make the chilli beans first. Warm the olive oil in a medium pan, add the onion and cook for 10 minutes over a medium heat until soft, then add the garlic, chillies and paprika and cook for a further 2 minutes. Add the tomatoes, honey, vinegar, beans and 200ml of water and season well. Reduce the heat to low and let it bubble away for at least 30 minutes, until the beans are soft and the sauce has reduced a little. Taste and adjust the seasoning.

To make the batter for the pancakes, blitz the spelt flakes in a food processor or blender to a coarse flour (you can skip this step if you are using spelt flour). Add the baking powder and a pinch of salt and pepper and blitz briefly to mix all the dry ingredients together. Add the eggs, and with the motor running, pour in the milk and add the oil, spinach and parsley. Blend until you get a lovely green colour and all the ingredients are incorporated into a smooth batter.

Heat a little oil in a waffle maker and pour in 8 tablespoons of the batter. Cook for 6–8 minutes, then remove and keep warm while you cook the rest of the waffles. Serve with a generous portion of the chilli beans, scattering both with the fresh herbs. Add an egg if you're really hungry.

Black Sticky Rice and Coconut Porridge

This glutinous black rice is so unique. Equally rich in colour and in flavour, it's almost too good to be true and like rye it can take a lot of spices. This recipe is a basic one but feel free to go rogue when it comes to loading it up with flavour – try pairing it with ginger for a warming, fresh kick.

• SERVES 2

FOR THE PORRIDGE
50g Chinese black sticky
   rice, soaked overnight
250ml coconut milk
½ vanilla pod
Pinch of sea salt

TO SERVE
1 tablespoon coconut
   palm sugar
1 passion fruit, halved, seeds
   and pulp scooped out
1 banana, sliced
2 teaspoons pomegranate
   seeds
2 teaspoons sesame
   seeds, toasted

• Rinse the soaked rice thoroughly, running it under the cold tap until the water runs as clear as possible. Add the rice and 250ml of water to a pan and cook over a medium heat for 10–15 minutes, until all the water has been absorbed.

Add the coconut milk, vanilla pod and sea salt and continue to cook for a further 10–15 minutes until it has a porridge-like consistency. Meanwhile, prepare the toppings.

Pour the rice porridge into 2 bowls and top with coconut palm sugar, passion fruit, banana, pomegranate seeds and sesame seeds.

This can be served hot, or left to cool and served as a delicious pudding in the summer.

Brunch Box

• SERVES 8, GENEROUSLY

FOR THE BLACK QUINOA SALAD
200g black quinoa, rinsed well and
    soaked in water for 30 minutes
2 spring onions, finely sliced
Large handful of toasted cashews

FOR THE TORTILLA
100ml olive oil, plus 2 tablespoons
2 onions, finely chopped
2 large garlic cloves,
    finely chopped
800g sweet potatoes, peeled
    and sliced into 5mm discs
Sea salt and black pepper
250g spinach, washed
8 large eggs

FOR THE BABY BASIL TOMATOES
400g cherry tomatoes, halved
2 tablespoons extra-virgin olive oil
Handful of basil leaves, torn
Sea salt and black pepper

FOR THE SALAD DRESSING
3 tablespoons extra-virgin olive oil
1½ tablespoons apple
    cider vinegar
1 teaspoon Dijon mustard
1 teaspoon honey
½ garlic clove, crushed
Squeeze of lemon juice

TO SERVE
2 ripe avocados, peeled, pitted
    and sliced
2 tablespoons black sesame seeds
Handful of alfalfa sprouts (optional)

This brunch box has so many different elements that when it's served together, it's a mega meal. It tastes amazing served warm, but is just as good cold, wrapped up and eaten on the go. You could also make up larger quantities and serve each part of the dish separately for a party or picnic. It's impossible to single out a favourite element from this combo. Perhaps that's why they've all ended up together. The tortilla is sweet and moreish, the quinoa creamy and crunchy, the tomatoes with olive oil and basil almost melting like butter. It's impossible to choose just one, so I'll have them all please!

• Drain and rinse the quinoa well and place in a pan with 335ml of water. Bring to the boil over a medium-high heat. Cook, uncovered, for 15 minutes, before reducing the heat to low, covering with a lid and cooking for a further 15 minutes, until all the water has been absorbed. Take off the heat and leave to rest with the lid on for a further 5 minutes, before removing the lid and leaving it to cool.

While the quinoa is cooking and cooling, prepare the tortilla. In a large frying pan, preferably ovenproof, warm 50ml of the olive oil over a medium heat and add the onions. Cook slowly for 10 minutes until completely soft and sweet, then stir in the remaining 50ml of oil, the garlic, sweet potatoes and a generous pinch of salt and pepper. Cover with a lid and continue cooking for further 10–15 minutes until the sweet potatoes are completely tender, stirring every few minutes so they don't catch.

Meanwhile, place the spinach in a large colander and pour over a kettle of boiling water to wilt it. When cool enough to handle, squeeze out any excess water.

Whisk the eggs in a large mixing bowl with a little seasoning, then stir the potato mix into the eggs, followed by the spinach, unravelling the clumps as you add it. Stir gently until everything is evenly distributed.

•——→

Clean the pan, then pour in the tortilla egg mix, then cover and cook very slowly for 20 minutes until the sides are cooked and coming away from the edge of the pan and the middle is not quite set. Remove from the hob and place under a hot grill uncovered for a final 4–5 minutes, watching it carefully so it doesn't burn. If your frying pan has a plastic handle, make sure it doesn't melt by covering it with kitchen foil. Set the tortilla aside to rest while you prepare the salads.

Combine the tomatoes, olive oil and basil together, then season well and set aside.

Combine the salad dressing ingredients in a small jar with a tight-fitting lid and give them a shake. Stir the spring onions, cashews and salad dressing into the cooled quinoa and season to taste.

Run a round-bladed knife around the edge of the tortilla to loosen it from the pan. Place a plate face down on the tortilla (make sure the plate is big enough to cover the whole tortilla), then flip the pan and the plate so that the tortilla comes out beautifully, ready for serving. Cut into slices, then serve with the quinoa, the cherry tomatoes and a few avocado slices. Scatter over the black sesame seeds and pinch of alfalfa sprouts before serving.

Sweet Potato Hash Browns with Chunky Avocado and Beetroot

Beetroot and sweet potato are wonderful because they're available all year round and can be used in so many ways, from hearty, warming dishes to light, vibrant salads. This simple recipe showcases the three main ingredients so that you can decipher each flavour individually; when combined together they create something really special. I love latkes (Jewish potato pancakes) and hash browns and wanted to come up with a different spin on them. Rolled oats bind these ones together without being too thick, while the avocado and alfafa sprouts on top add even more lightness. Finish with a squeeze of lemon juice for a nice lick of acidity. Feel free to mix up the root veg too – celeriac, parsnips and carrots all work wonderfully well.

- SERVES 4

FOR THE HASH
800g sweet potato, peeled
   and grated
2 medium eggs
½ onion, thinly sliced
80g rolled oats, blitzed
   to a coarse flour
   in a food processor
1 tablespoon olive oil
1 teaspoon sea salt
Black pepper
Olive oil, for frying

FOR THE CHUNKY AVOCADO
AND BEETROOT
2 ripe avocados, halved and
   cut into large chunks
4 cooked beetroot, cut into
   large chunks
2 tablespoons extra-virgin
   olive oil
Juice of ½ lemon
200g alfalfa sprouts, micro
   beetroot cress or rocket
   (or any salad of your choice)

- Place the grated sweet potato in a colander, rinse under cold water, then squeeze out as much liquid as possible with your hands.

Beat the eggs in a large bowl and then add the onion, blitzed oats, olive oil, salt, pepper and sweet potato and mix well with your hands.

Add a splash of olive oil to a non-stick frying pan over a medium-high heat. When hot, add 2 tablespoons of the mixture for each hash brown and press down with the back of a spoon to make a 10cm circle. (You will probably need to cook these in two batches, depending on the size of your pan.)

Cover the pan with lid and cook each side for 3 minutes until golden and cooked through. They may take a little longer, or cook a little quicker, depending on the size of your hash brown and how finely the potato has been grated. Keep warm in a low oven while you prepare the salad.

Combine the avocados and beetroot in a bowl, season well and dress with the olive oil and lemon juice before gently tossing. Place a mound of the salad on top of the hash browns and top with a crack of black pepper and a small handful of sprouts or cress/salad leaves.

LUNCH

Red Rice Bowl with Marinated Kale and Beetroot Hummus

This dish evolved from a Sunday leftovers session, but soon became a regular staple. The red rice is so nutty and adds a great richness that carries the whole dish. I love how the silky beetroot hummus and avocado contrast with the crunch and sharpness of the radish and sauerkraut. If you are unable to find red rice, replace with either wild rice or brown rice.

• SERVES 2

FOR THE RICE

50g red rice, soaked for
　½ hour and rinsed well
　(or use brown or wild rice)
Olive oil
6 radishes, finely sliced
1 small ripe avocado, peeled,
　pitted and chopped
1–2 tablespoons sauerkraut,
　homemade or from a jar
　(optional)
2 soft-boiled eggs

FOR THE MARINATED KALE

1 tablespoon tahini
1 tablespoon tamari
1 tablespoon extra-virgin olive oil
1 tablespoon apple cider vinegar
Juice of ½ lime
150g kale, stems discarded,
　leaves shredded

FOR THE BEETROOT HUMMUS

1 garlic clove, crushed with
　a little sea salt
400g can of chickpeas,
　drained and rinsed
250g cooked beetroot
2 tablespoon tahini
4 tablespoons extra-virgin
　olive oil or walnut oil
Juice of 1 lemon

• Place the rice in a pan and pour over 250ml of boiling water. Bring to the boil, then reduce the heat and simmer for about 45 minutes, or until just tender. Drain and leave to cool.

Meanwhile, make the marinade for the kale by whisking together the tahini, tamari, oil, vinegar and lime juice. It may seem a little thick and lumpy, but don't worry. Add the kale and scrunch together with your hands so every bit is covered in dressing and it starts to soften.

Make the hummus next. Place the garlic, chickpeas, beetroot and tahini in a food processor and blend until coarse. With the motor running, slowly pour in the oil until smooth, then squeeze in the lemon juice and season well. Transfer to a bowl.

Drizzle a little olive oil over the cooled rice and season with salt. Stir in the radishes, avocado and marinated kale and pile into bowls. Top with the hummus, sauerkraut and soft-boiled eggs.

Buckwheat Tabbouleh

Tabbouleh is such a crowd-pleaser. It is usually made with bulgur wheat, but I find the buckwheat adds an earthy, nutty tone that complements the fresh kick of parsley and lemon. If you happen to have a crowd, rope them into helping you with this simple dish and it'll be ready in 5 minutes. Serve with hummus, halloumi, Spelt Pittas (see page 90) and roasted red peppers.

- **SERVES 4 AS A SIDE**

25g buckwheat groats, soaked in cold water for 1 hour
2 large ripe tomatoes, finely chopped
Bunch of parsley, leaves picked and finely chopped
Handful of mint leaves, finely chopped
½ red onion, finely chopped
Juice of ½ lemon, plus extra if needed
3 tablespoons extra-virgin olive oil
Sea salt and black pepper

- Rinse and drain the buckwheat and place it in a small pan with 125ml of water. Bring to the boil, then reduce the heat to a simmer and cook for 12–15 minutes, or until just tender and most of the water has been absorbed. Remove from the heat, cover with a lid and leave to stand for 5 minutes to dry out a little.

Drain and rinse the buckwheat in fresh water and then transfer to a large bowl along with the remaining ingredients. Season to taste with salt and pepper and add a little more lemon juice if you think it needs it; it should be very perky.

Quinoa and Freekeh Summer Salad

Sometimes too much of one grain can be overpowering in a dish, so here is a wonderful recipe where the lightness of quinoa and the richness of freekeh really complement each other well to make a beautiful summer salad.

• SERVES 4

75g whole quinoa, rinsed
   well and soaked in water for
   30 minutes
75g freekeh, rinsed well
   and soaked in water for
   at least 1 hour
50g pine nuts, lightly toasted
150g carrots, grated
150g pomegranate seeds
200g feta
Finely grated zest of
   1 unwaxed orange
Handful of mint leaves, chopped
Handful of parsley leaves,
   chopped

FOR THE DRESSING
4 tablespoons extra-virgin olive oil
1 tablespoon red wine vinegar
1½ tablespoons pomegranate
   molasses
1 garlic clove, crushed
Juice of ½ lemon
Sea salt and black pepper

• Rinse and drain the quinoa and the freekeh and place in a medium pan. Add 500ml of water and bring to the boil. Reduce the heat to a simmer and cook, covered, for 12–15 minutes. Turn off the heat and set aside to cool.

Prepare the dressing by whisking together all the ingredients in a bowl until well combined (or shake in a jar with a tight-fitting lid).

Mix the pine nuts, grated carrot, pomegranate seeds, feta, orange zest, mint and parsley into the cooled grain mix. Pour over 4–6 tablespoons of the dressing, taste and adjust the seasoning and serve with some salad leaves.

Beetroot and Chickpea Falafel

These falafels are a great twist on a classic. The beetroot has a great tone and sweetness to it against the rich outer crust of rough rye. They're great to serve with a salad or for a big table to share. Make sure you season them well as you go.

• MAKES 12–14

2 tablespoons olive oil
½ onion, finely chopped
1 garlic clove, finely chopped
1 teaspoon cumin seeds
400g can of chickpeas,
   drained and rinsed
Large handful of coriander leaves
60g raw beetroot, grated and
   wrung out in kitchen paper
1½ teaspoons of sea salt
Juice of ½ lemon
1 medium egg beaten with
   a splash of whole/oat milk
125g rye flakes, blitzed in a food
   processor to coarse crumbs
500ml coconut oil, for frying
Sweet pickled chillies, to serve

• Warm a little of the olive oil in a small pan over a medium heat and gently fry the onion for 8 minutes until soft, then add the garlic and the cumin seeds and cook for a further minute or so. Stir in the chickpeas and cook for 3–4 minutes to dry them out a little, then season to taste.

Place the chickpea mixture, coriander, beetroot, remaining olive oil, 1½ teaspoons of sea salt, crack of black pepper and lemon juice in a food processor or blender and blitz until smooth. Transfer to a bowl, taste and adjust the seasoning.

Preheat the oven to 200°C/fan 180°C/400°F/gas mark 6. Place the beaten egg mix and rye flakes in separate shallow bowls.

Make the falafel by rolling the mixture into small walnut-sized balls with your hands. Dip each in the egg mix and then roll in the rye flakes. Place in the fridge while you prepare the others.

Spoon the coconut oil into a small pan so that it comes at least 2cm up the sides. Place over a medium heat and warm up until it reaches 160°C (if you don't have a cooking thermometer, test by dropping in a cube of bread; when it turns golden the oil is ready). Fry the falafel, one at a time, for 2–3 minutes until golden brown, turning them frequently. Remove from the pan with a slotted spoon and transfer to a baking tray while you fry the rest of the falafel. Pop the tray into the oven and cook for a further 8 minutes. Allow them to cool slightly before serving with pickled chillies.

Spelt Salad with Beetroot, Feta, Chickpea and Apple

Spelt has a deep, earthy taste that reminds me of beetroot. So it felt like a no-brainer to serve them together. Roasted beetroot is sweet and velvety; I definitely prefer it to boiled beetroot. If you don't have time to roast the beetroot you can use cooked beetroot – just make sure you cut into small, matchstick-sized pieces, or coarsely grate it. Toss with sharp feta, sweet apples and peppery rocket for a simple, breezy salad.

• SERVES 4

4 small beetroot (about 300g), scrubbed (or use ready-cooked beetroot, see recipe introduction)
1 tablespoon olive oil
85g pearled spelt, soaked in water for at least 30 minutes
½ teaspoon sea salt
100g feta, crumbled
½ × 400g can of chickpeas, drained and rinsed
50g rocket
1 red apple, thinly sliced

FOR THE DRESSING
3 tablespoons extra-virgin olive oil
1 tablespoon apple cider vinegar
¼ teaspoon ground cinnamon (optional)
½ teaspoon honey
1 teaspoon Dijon mustard
½ garlic clove, crushed with a little sea salt
Juice of ½ lemon

• Preheat the oven to 200°C/fan 180°C/400°F/gas mark 6.

Place the beetroot in a small roasting tray and rub them all over with the olive oil. Bake in the oven for 1–1½ hours (depending on the size of your beetroot), or until soft.

Drain and rinse the soaked spelt, place in a medium pan along with 500ml of water and the salt and bring to the boil. Reduce the heat and leave to bubble away for about 20 minutes, or until tender. Drain and leave to cool.

Meanwhile, make the dressing by combining all the ingredients in a bowl or jar with a tight-fitting lid and whisking or shaking to combine.

Once the beetroot has cooled, peel and roughly chop and then combine in a large bowl with the cooled spelt and all the remaining ingredients in a large bowl. Pour over dressing to serve.

Orange and Radicchio Freekeh with Black Olive Tapenade

This salad is wonderfully bright and light – perfect on a hot day – but you can just as easily source these ingredients in the middle of winter. They'll bring a welcome freshness to months of broths and stews.

• SERVES 2

50g freekeh, rinsed well
and soaked in water for
at least 1 hour
Sea salt and black pepper
3 tablespoons olive oil
1 tablespoon pomegranate
molasses
1 head of radicchio, leaves
torn and washed
1 orange, peeled and sliced
2 tablespoons black
olive tapenade
Few sprigs of dill

FOR THE BLACK OLIVE TAPENADE
100g black olives, pitted
and finely chopped
1 teaspoon capers, rinsed and
roughly chopped
½ red chilli, finely chopped
(deseed if you prefer less heat)
Handful of parsley leaves,
finely chopped
½ garlic clove, crushed
with a little sea salt
1 tablespoon red wine vinegar
Juice of ½ lemon
3–4 tablespoons extra-virgin
olive oil

• Drain the soaked freekeh and rinse well under cold water. Add to a pan without any water and lightly cook the grains over a medium heat, stirring the pan, until they ever so slightly start to toast, then add 250ml of water and ½ teaspoon sea salt. Bring to the boil, then reduce the heat to a simmer and cook for 20 minutes, adding a little more water if it begins to dry out. Leave to cool.

Meanwhile, make the tapenade by combining the ingredients together in a bowl. Season to taste with black pepper; you shouldn't need to add salt as the olives already have a salty flavour. If you prefer a slightly finer tapenade, place all the ingredients in a food processor and blend until smooth.

Whisk the olive oil and pomegranate molasses together in the bottom of a salad bowl. Add the freekeh, radicchio leaves and orange slices. Season well, then toss together and divide between 2 plates. Top with the tapenade and dill and serve.

Rye Panzanella

From June to October, when tomatoes are in season, England bursts at the seams with varieties in every shape, size and colour. Rye bread, roughly torn and then toasted until crisp, not only adds a rich malt flavour to the dish but also serves to soak up all the juices that pool at the bottom. The refreshing cucumber and salty capers contrast beautifully with the juicy tomatoes and toasted bread.

- SERVES 4

200g fresh or stale rye bread,
  crusts removed
200g mix of ripe seasonal
  tomatoes (red, yellow, blood,
  heritage), chopped
½ red onion, thinly sliced
1 ripe avocado, peeled, pitted
  and chopped into chunks
½ cucumber, chopped
  into chunks
1 tablespoon capers, rinsed
Handful of basil leaves
½ garlic clove, crushed with
  a little sea salt
4 tablespoons extra-virgin
  olive oil
1½ tablespoons red wine vinegar
Sea salt and black pepper

- Preheat the oven to 200°C/fan 180°C/400°F/gas 6. Tear the rye bread into small chunks and spread over a baking tray. Bake for 10–15 minutes until it starts to crisp up and turn golden at the edges.

Mix together the rest of the ingredients in a large bowl. When the rye is ready, throw it in and make sure it gets a good coating in all the juices.

Aubergine with Green Beans and Freekeh

• SERVES 2

50g freekeh, rinsed well
  and soaked in water for
  at least 1 hour
Sea salt and black pepper
1 small garlic clove, crushed
  with a little sea salt
4–5 tablespoons olive oil
1 small aubergine, cut into
  2–3cm chunks
150g green beans, topped
  and tailed
1 teaspoon nigella seeds
1 teaspoon black mustard seeds
½ teaspoon coriander seeds,
  lightly crushed
Juice of ½ lemon
½ fresh red chilli, deseeded
  and thinly sliced
Seeds from ½ pomegranate
2 tablespoons Greek-style
  yogurt, to serve

I love aubergines but I know not everyone feels the same – even in my family it divides people 50:50. It's what I'd describe as quite a meaty vegetable – tender on the inside but hearty and robust on the outside, the yielding texture giving it a bit more bite. Freshness and depth is added to this salad by the freekeh – young, golden-green wheat that has been toasted; it's somewhat grassy in taste, but also rich and almost smoky. Top with barely cooked green beans for some additional crunch and you'll have even the most staunch aubergine opponent coming back for more.

• Drain and rinse the freekeh well under cold water. Add to a pan without any water and lightly cook the grains over a medium heat, stirring the pan, until they ever so slightly start to toast, then add 250ml of water and ½ teaspoon sea salt. Bring to the boil, then reduce the heat to a simmer and cook for 20 minutes, adding a little more water if it begins to dry out.

Mix the garlic with 2 tablespoons of the oil and rub into the aubergine. Warm 1 tablespoon of oil in a pan over a medium-high heat and fry the aubergine for 5–6 minutes, shaking the pan frequently and adding another tablespoon of oil if it needs it, until dark golden brown, soft and cooked through. Season with a little salt and keep warm.

Meanwhile, bring a pan of water to the boil with a pinch of salt and cook the beans for a couple of minutes until tender, then drain.

Place the nigella seeds, mustard seeds, coriander seeds, lemon juice, remaining tablespoon of oil and chilli in a large mixing bowl and season well. Once the aubergine is cooked, add to the mixing bowl along with the freekeh, green beans and pomegranate seeds and toss well.

Transfer to plates and dollop over a little yogurt before serving.

Seared Tuna and
Black Quinoa Salad

Tuna is such a unique fish, both in the way it tastes and with its distinct colouring and texture. In this dish I've kept the tuna simple, just coating with a light seasoning of flaked sea salt and sesame seeds, which toast slightly as you cook the fish. The black quinoa adds a fresh bite and carries the ginger, chilli and lime dressing beautifully for a great accompaniment to the fish.

- SERVES 2

100g black quinoa (or use
  white quinoa), rinsed well and
  soaked in water for 30 minutes
2 × 150g tuna steaks
50g white and/or black
  sesame seeds
2 tablespoons olive oil
2 tablespoons sesame oil
Small handful of coriander leaves,
  roughly chopped

FOR THE PEANUT SAUCE
½ garlic clove
50g coconut palm sugar
  (or use soft dark brown sugar)
200g unsalted peanuts, roasted
1–2 Thai red chillies (deseed
  if you prefer less heat)
1 tablespoon kecap manis
  (Indonesian sweet soy sauce)
  or regular soy sauce, plus
  extra if needed
Sea salt, to taste
Juice of 4 limes, plus extra
  if needed

FOR THE DRESSING
1 tablespoon freshly grated
  root ginger
2 tablespoons sesame oil
2 tablespoons tamari
Juice of 1 lime
4 spring onions, finely chopped
1 fresh red chilli, thinly sliced
  (deseed if you prefer less heat)

- Rinse and drain the quinoa, place in a pan with 500ml of water and bring to the boil. Cook, uncovered, for 15 minutes, before reducing the heat to low, covering with a lid and cooking for a further 15 minutes, until all the water has been absorbed. Remove from the heat, drain if necessary, then return to the pan and leave to rest with the lid on for a further 5 minutes before removing the lid and leaving it to cool.

Next make the peanut sauce. Place the garlic, coconut palm sugar, roasted peanuts, chillies, kecap manis and salt (if you are using regular soy sauce you won't need to add salt here) in a blender and blitz to a rough paste. Add the lime juice and up to 100ml of water. Once you have a nice spoonable sauce, stop blending, taste and adjust the seasoning with more kecap manis or lime juice, if needed.

Make the dressing by whisking together the ginger, sesame oil, tamari, lime juice, spring onions and chilli. Mix the dressing into the cooled quinoa.

Season the tuna with salt on both sides. Spread the sesame seeds out over a dish and then press both sides of the tuna steaks in them to coat.

Warm the olive and sesame oil in a frying pan over a medium-high heat. Once nice and hot, add the tuna steaks to the pan, searing each side for 30 seconds.

Divide the quinoa between 2 plates. Slice the tuna steaks into 1cm slices and lay them over the top of the grains. Spoon a few dollops of peanut sauce over each serving and top with a good sprinkling of coriander.

Mackerel, Beetroot and Crispy Quinoa

This dish doesn't need much explanation – it's just a lovely combination of some of my favourite ingredients. The light, crisp quinoa mixed with sweet beetroot and apple works well with the strong, smoky tones of the mackerel. Keep it fresh with a good helping of dill and add a little spicy heat with the horseradish dressing.

- SERVES 2

½ red onion, sliced into
  thin crescents
2 tablespoons balsamic vinegar
1 tablespoon honey
2 black peppercorns
75g whole white quinoa, rinsed
  well and soaked in water for
  30 minutes
4 tablespoons olive oil
230g smoked mackerel fillets,
  flaked
250g cooked beetroot,
  roughly chopped
½ red apple, thinly sliced
  or coarsely grated
Handful of fresh dill, roughly
  torn from the stem

FOR THE DRESSING
1½ teaspoons creamed
  horseradish
Juice of ½ lemon
1 tablespoon olive oil
Sea salt and black pepper

- Start by lightly pickling the red onions. Put the onions in a jar or bowl with 2 tablespoons of boiling water, the balsamic vinegar, honey and black peppercorns. Set aside for 20 minutes.

Rinse and drain the quinoa and put in a medium pan with 250ml of water. Place over a medium heat and bring to the boil, then reduce the heat to a simmer and cook, covered, for 12–15 minutes. Set aside to cool and fully dry out.

Meanwhile whisk together all the ingredients for the dressing in a bowl.

When the quinoa has fully dried out, heat the olive oil in a pan and allow it to get really hot. Start adding the quinoa, half a cup at a time, and cook in the oil for 2–3 minutes, allowing it to crisp and turn golden – take care here as the quinoa might spit.

Drain the pickled red onion. Mix together the crispy quinoa, pickled onion, smoked mackerel, beetroot, apple and dill with a crack of black pepper. Divide between 2 plates and serve with a good drizzle of horseradish dressing.

Trout with Sorrel, Fennel and Spelt Risotto

SERVES 4

2 tablespoons olive oil
2 banana shallots, thinly sliced
2 garlic cloves, thinly sliced
1 fennel bulb, trimmed and
    thinly sliced
1 teaspoon fennel seeds
400g pearled spelt, soaked
    in water for 30 minutes
1 glass of white wine
1.2 litres vegetable stock
350g sorrel, roughly chopped
    (or use spinach, see above)
Finely grated zest and juice
    of ½ unwaxed lemon
Sea salt and black pepper

FOR THE TROUT
Olive oil, for drizzling
4 rainbow trout fillets,
    about 160g each
4 sprigs of thyme
4 lemon slices
2 tablespoons capers, rinsed

In September, my boyfriend Dom and I flew to Salzburg with our bikes and cycled across Bavaria to Zurich. Cycling more than 100km each day left us ravenous. We were able to get through the day on snacks, but by dinner we needed something pretty hearty to prepare us for the next day of cycling. It was all made worth it when we'd park near a lake and order a trout – we had a healthy rotation of bratwurst, sauerkraut and lemony trout for the duration of the trip. This recipe is comforting, but not too heavy. If you can't find sorrel, try replacing it with spinach (which is less peppery) and a little extra lemon juice.

- Add the olive oil to a pan over a medium heat. Add the shallots and soften for 6–8 minutes before adding the garlic, fennel and fennel seeds; cook for a further 3 minutes.

Drain the spelt, then stir into the vegetables and pour over the wine. Bring to the boil and cook for 3 minutes, then reduce the heat and start slowly adding the stock every 10 minutes or so, until you've used all the stock up and the spelt has softened and become sticky. Once the spelt is cooked through, add the sorrel and lemon zest and juice and season with salt and pepper.

Preheat the oven to 200°C/fan 180°C/400°F/gas mark 6. Drizzle a baking tray with a little oil, then lay out the trout fillets, skin side-up. Top each one with a sprig of thyme, a lemon slice, a drizzle of olive oil and a little seasoning. Bake for 15 minutes until just cooked.

Divide the risotto between 4 plates and top with the trout fillets. Scatter ½ tablespoon of capers and a good crack of black pepper over each one, drizzle with olive oil and serve.

Sea Bass with Tomato, Aubergine and Pearl Barley

It would be a cliché to say how much I was affected by a week I spent in Italy a few summers ago. But the place is full of clichés for a reason. The simplest of dishes, whether fresh pasta or a bowl of lightly seasoned tomatoes and basil, were among the most memorable. Most of the menus included a tomato and aubergine dish, usually as a parmigiana, and I could never resist. Here, aubergine and tomatoes create their own buttery, sweet and refreshing juice, which is soaked up by the plump barley. A lovely combination for a fresh, white fish.

• SERVES 2

3 tablespoons olive oil
1 garlic clove, crushed
   with a little sea salt
Sea salt and black pepper
1 aubergine, cut into
   2–3cm cubes
200g cherry tomatoes
2 sea bass fillets,
   about 160g each
30g pine nuts, toasted
Small handful of parsley leaves,
   finely chopped
Juice of ½ lemon, to serve

FOR THE PEARL BARLEY
1 tablespoon olive oil
½ onion, thinly sliced
75g pearl barley, rinsed
375ml hot vegetable stock

• Preheat the oven to 180°C/fan 160°C/350°F/gas mark 4.

Mix 2 tablespoons of the olive oil, the crushed garlic and some seasoning together in a bowl, then add the aubergine and tomatoes and toss to make sure every bit is nicely coated. Spread out over a baking tray then place in the oven for 40–45 minutes, or until the aubergine is coloured and softened and the tomatoes have started to wrinkle.

Meanwhile, prepare the pearl barley. Heat the olive oil in a pan over a medium heat and gently fry the onion until soft, about 8 minutes. Stir in the barley, then pour in the stock. Bring to the boil, then turn down to a simmer and cook for 40 minutes until tender and the stock has been absorbed. Season well.

Towards the end of the cooking time, season the sea bass fillets on both sides with salt. Warm the remaining tablespoon of olive oil in a frying pan over a medium-high heat, then add the fish, skin-side down and fry for 3–4 minutes until the skin is golden and the fish is almost cooked. Turn and cook the other side for 1–2 minutes, depending on the thickness of the fillet.

Once the barley and the roasted veg are ready, tip the aubergine and tomatoes into the barley, folding them in gently so as not to squish them too much.

Divide the barley between 2 plates, sit the sea bass fillets on top and sprinkle with the pine nuts and parsley. Add a good squeeze of lemon juice over the fish before serving.

Salmon with Red Quinoa and Chilli Pak Choy

I've been told that pink and red clash. But here the pink salmon and red quinoa work perfectly, so I'm refuting those claims. I'm rather partial to pak choy and believe there's no such thing as too much of it, so be generous when serving. This is a quick and easy dish to make for lunch.

• SERVES 4

100g red quinoa (or use white quinoa), rinsed well and soaked in water for 30 minutes
1 tablespoon sesame oil
2 tablespoons tamari
2 tablespoons honey
1 teaspoon freshly grated root ginger
Juice of ½ lime
4 salmon fillets, about 160g each

FOR THE CHILLI PAK CHOY
2 tablespoons sesame oil
4 spring onions, thinly sliced
1 garlic clove, thinly sliced
1 red chilli, thinly sliced (deseed if you prefer less heat)
1 teaspoon freshly grated root ginger
600g pak choy
1 teaspoon tamari
1 teaspoon fish sauce

• Make the quinoa first. Drain and rinse the quinoa, place in a pan with 500ml of water and bring to the boil. Cook, uncovered, for 25 minutes, adding a little extra water if needed. Remove from the heat, drain away any water (most of it will have been absorbed), then return to the pan and leave to rest, covered, for 10 minutes before removing the lid and leaving it to cool.

Preheat the oven to 200°C/fan 180°C/400°F/gas mark 6. Combine the sesame oil, tamari, honey, ginger and lime juice in a small baking dish, then add the salmon and rub the marinade all over. Leave to marinate for 15 minutes, then pop into the oven, skin-side up, and bake for 8–10 minutes, or until just cooked.

To make the chilli pak choy, warm the sesame oil in a wok or wide pan over a medium-high heat. Add the spring onions, garlic, chilli and ginger and cook, stirring, for 2 minutes. Stir in the pak choy so it's nicely coated, then add a splash of water, place a lid on top and cook for a further 2 minutes. Stir the cooked quinoa into the pak choy, then add the tamari and fish sauce and allow to heat through.

Divide the quinoa and pak choy between 4 plates and top with the baked salmon. Drizzle over any juices and serve.

Slow-roast Pork with Spelt and Pomegranate Slaw

Who doesn't get excited at the prospect of a roast? There's always too much food, which allows for last-minute additions in the form of hungry friends. This roast is perfect for all seasons – the juicy spelt, light blend of raw vegetables and herbs in the slaw can make it both hearty and refreshing. Pop the pork in the oven and leave it for at least 4 hours to ensure a really tender and delicious roast.

- SERVES 10

4kg pork shoulder, skin removed and scored about 1cm apart
2 onions, peeled and thickly sliced
2 tablespoons red wine vinegar
Sea salt

FOR THE RUB
3 tablespoons honey
2 tablespoons olive oil
1 teaspoon chilli flakes
2 teaspoons sea salt
2 teaspoons ground cumin
1 teaspoon ground cinnamon

FOR THE SPELT SLAW
100g pearled spelt
½ teaspoon sea salt
½ red cabbage, finely shredded
3 carrots, peeled and shredded
Handful of mint leaves, chopped
2 tablespoons olive oil
Juice of 1 lemon
1 teaspoon Dijon mustard
Seeds from ½ pomegranate

- Preheat the oven to its highest setting. Place the scored pork skin, uncovered, in the fridge to dry out.

Mix together the ingredients for the rub and then massage into the pork. Spread the onion slices out in a roasting tray and sit the pork on top. Place in the oven for 30 minutes, turning the meat over after 15 minutes. Reduce the oven temperature to 160°C/fan 140°C/325°F/gas mark 3 and continue to cook for a further 4–5 hours (cooking times for pork vary a bit), turning it over and basting it with the pan juices occasionally. After about 4 hours you should be able to easily pull off a bit of meat; if not, return to the oven for a little longer.

Meanwhile, place the spelt in a pan and pour over 500ml of water. Bring to the boil and cook for 20 minutes until all the water is absorbed. Season with the salt and leave to cool.

Take the pork out of the oven, remove the pork skin and set aside, and sprinkle over the vinegar over the meat. Cover with foil and then a tea towel and leave to rest. Meanwhile increase the oven temerature to 220°C/fan 200°C/425°F/gas mark 7. Place the pork skin on a wire rack over a baking tray and place on the top shelf of the oven for 30 minutes, checking on it regularly. Remove from the oven when the skin has crackled and sprinkle generously with sea salt. Shred the meat with a couple of forks and toss it in the resting juices in the roasting tray, then slice up the crackling.

Meanwhile, combine the red cabbage and carrots with the mint, olive oil, lemon juice and mustard. Once everything is well combined, stir in the pomegranate seeds.

To serve, pile up the spelt slaw on a large serving platter and top with the shredded pork and crackling.

Smørrebrød

How many ways can you make a smørrebrød? Far more than four, as evidenced by Torverhallerne food market in Copenhagen. This market distracted me no end as I surveyed their range of colourful smørrebrød. These recipes are a great starting point from which you can go on to be as creative as you like.

CUCUMBER, SOFT CHEESE, RADISH

• SERVES 1

1 slice of rye bread
1 teaspoon olive oil
Sea salt and black pepper
½ cucumber, thinly sliced
1–2 tablespoons soft cheese
2 radishes, thinly sliced

• Drizzle the slice of rye bread with the olive oil and add a sprinkling of salt. Layer the slices of cucumber on top of the bread, followed by a dollop of soft cheese. Scatter over the radishes and season well with salt and freshly ground black pepper.

•⟶

PICKLED HERRING, BEETROOT, HORSERADISH, PEA SHOOTS

• SERVES 2

1 medium cooked beetroot
1 tablespoon Greek-style yogurt
¼ teaspoon white wine vinegar
1 teaspoon fresh horseradish, grated
 (or use creamed horseradish)
1 teaspoon olive oil
100g pickled herring, chopped
 (rollmops)
Squeeze of lemon juice
Sea salt and black pepper
2 slices of rye bread
Pea shoots (optional)

• Mix together the beetroot, yogurt, white wine vinegar, horseradish, olive oil, herring, lemon juice and salt and pepper in a bowl until everything is evenly combined. Pile on top of the rye bread slices and garnish with some refreshing pea shoots, if using.

FIG, MOZZARELLA, MINT

• SERVES 1

1 slice of rye bread
2 teaspoons olive oil
Sea salt and black pepper
25g buffalo mozzarella, torn
3–4 mint leaves, roughly chopped
1 ripe fig, sliced
Alfalfa sprouts (optional)

• Drizzle the slice of rye bread with a
teaspoon of olive oil and add a
sprinkling of salt. Layer the torn
mozzarella, mint and sliced fig on top
and drizzle over a little more olive oil.
Season with salt and a good crack of
black pepper and top with some
alfalfa sprouts.

•——→

EGG, RED ONION

• SERVES 1

1 medium egg
1 slice of rye bread
Butter, for spreading
¼ small red onion, thinly sliced
Small handful of dill, roughly torn
Sea salt and black pepper

• Bring a medium pan of water to
the boil, add the egg and boil for
7 minutes. Drain and immediately
run under cold water until cool
enough to peel. Cut the egg into thin
rings. Spread the rye bread with
a good helping of top-quality butter.
Layer the bread with the sliced egg,
red onion, dill and a good sprinkling
of salt and black pepper.

•——→

Oat Scotch Eggs
with Pickled Cucumber

I've been quite taken by the rise of the Scotch egg. This recipe is a breeze and will impress any guest. The secret is in using the very best ingredients: fresh organic, free-range eggs for deep orange, oozy yolks and grass-fed organic sausagemeat for flavour. Don't forget the pickled cucumber, you'd be missing out if you did.

• MAKES 5

6 medium eggs, at room
   temperature, 1 beaten
   with a splash of whole/oat milk
500g sausagemeat
3 spring onions, finely chopped
Small handful of parsley leaves,
   chopped
1 garlic clove, crushed
   with a little sea salt
1 tablespoon Dijon mustard
100g rolled oats
About 500ml coconut oil

FOR THE PICKLED CUCUMBER
1 cucumber, thinly sliced
   into thin rounds
½ white onion, thinly sliced
1 tablespoon sea salt
120ml apple cider vinegar
1 tablespoon honey
1 teaspoon yellow mustard seeds
1 teaspoon black peppercorns
1 clove

• Make the pickled cucumber first by mixing the cucumber and onion together with the salt. Leave for 10 minutes to draw out the liquid and then rinse away the salt and excess liquid. Drain thoroughly. In a small pan, heat the vinegar, honey, mustard seeds, peppercorns and clove until it just comes to the boil. Remove from the heat, add the cucumber and onion to the hot liquid and set aside, covered, to cool.

Bring a pan of water to the boil, place in the eggs and simmer for 6 minutes for soft-boiled (or 7 minutes for hard-boiled). Once cooked, drain and immediately run under cold water until cool enough to handle, then peel. Leave the eggs in a bowl of cold water until you're ready to roll them.

Mix the sausagemeat, spring onions, parsley, garlic and mustard together in a bowl and season with sea salt and black pepper. Mix well with your hands so everything is completely incorporated.

Preheat the oven to 200°C/fan 180°C/400°F/gas mark 6. Place the oats and beaten egg mix in separate shallow bowls.

Start building the Scotch eggs: divide the sausagemeat mixture into five equal portions and pat each one into a circle about 8mm thick and 12.5cm in diameter. Place an egg in the middle of one circle and carefully start to wrap the sausage around the egg. Dip the wrapped egg into the beaten egg mix, and then roll in the oats. Place in the fridge while you prepare the others.

•⟶

Place the coconut oil in a small pan with high sides so that it comes at least 2cm up the edges of the pan. Start to bring up the temperature of oil over a medium heat until it reaches 160°C (if you don't have a cooking thermometer, test by dropping in a cube of bread; when it turns golden the oil is ready). Fry the Scotch eggs, one at a time, for 2–3 minutes, turning them frequently and spooning the oil over the top of the egg until golden brown. Remove from the pan with a slotted spoon and transfer to a baking tray while you fry the rest of the eggs. Pop the eggs into the oven for a further 7 minutes, then remove and allow to cool for a few minutes.

Use a sharp knife to slice through the middle of each egg before serving with the pickled cucumber.

Green Buckwheat Wraps

The great thing about these wraps is that you can fill them with anything and everything to create many new and exciting recipes. Buckwheat is a pseudograin (a seed that behaves and has the same nutritional properties as a grain) with a unique taste and flavour, and I was keen to create something green and fresh with this recipe. Pack it really full and wrap it tight for an incredibly satisfying lunch.

SERVES 2

165g buckwheat flakes,
    blitzed in a food processor
    to a coarse flour
    (or use buckwheat flour)
Good pinch of sea salt
1 egg, beaten
1 tablespoon coconut
    or olive oil

TO SERVE
4 tablespoons hummus
2 avocados, peeled and roughly
    smashed with a fork
½ cucumber, cut into thin strips
100g spinach leaves
Small handful of basil leaves
4 tablespoons pine nuts,
    toasted
2 tablespoons shaved Parmesan
Extra-virgin olive oil
Squeeze of lemon juice

- Mix together the buckwheat and salt in a bowl. Create a well in the middle of the flour, add the egg and 375ml of water and whisk together to create a smooth batter.

Heat the oil in a non-stick frying pan and ladle in 120ml (about 8 tablespoons) of batter for each wrap, swirling the batter evenly over the base of the pan to create a thin pancake. Cook for 2 minutes until the underside of the wrap starts to golden. Flip over and cook the other side for a further 2 minutes. Continue with the remaining batter to make 1–2 more wraps, adding a little more oil if needed.

Fill each wrap with hummus, avocado, cucumber, spinach, basil, pine nuts, Parmesan, a drizzle of olive oil and a squeeze of lemon juice. Fold the ends of the wrap in by a couple of centimetres and then roll up the wrap. Slice each wrap in half and admire the beautiful green feast.

How to Build
a Pancake

Grains are incredibly versatile when it comes to pancakes, as they can be made either sweet or savoury. Simply choose your grain and 'glue' and follow the method opposite, adding additional texture and spices and topping with fruit, cream, extras and crunch to create your perfect pancake.

SWEET

GRAIN	GLUE	ADDITIONAL TEXTURE	SPICES
· Buckwheat (can be dry so combine 50:50 with rolled oats)	· Leftover porridge		· Ground cinnamon
	· Banana, mashed		· Ground cardamom
	· Sweet potato purée	· Cacao nibs	· Ground ginger
· Rolled oats	· Beetroot purée	· Whole millet	· Nutmeg
· Rye flour	· Carrot purée	· Popped quinoa	· Vanilla seeds
· Quinoa flakes	· Stewed apple	· Popped grains	· Ground turmeric
· Spelt flakes or flour	· Parsnip purée	· Fresh berries	· Chai
· Rice flakes	· Butternut squash purée		

GRAIN	GLUE	ADDITIONAL TEXTURE	SPICES
· Buckwheat (can be dry so combine 50:50 with rolled oats)	· Sweet potato purée	· Whole millet	· Ground cumin
	· Cooked spinach	· Popped quinoa	· Ground coriander
	· Beetroot purée	· Popped grains	· Chilli powder
· Rolled oats	· Cooked leeks		· Garlic powder
· Rye flour	· Carrot purée		· Black pepper
· Quinoa flakes	· Parsnip purée		· Mustard seeds
· Spelt flakes or flour			· Nutmeg
· Rice flakes			· Dried thyme
			· Ground turmeric
			· Chives
			· Parsley

SAVOURY

1 cup grains
1 cup 'glue'
4 medium eggs
1 teaspoon baking powder
Pinch of sea salt
1–2 tablespoons milk or water
1–2 tablespoons additional texture (optional)
¼–½ teaspoon spice (optional)
Coconut oil or unsalted butter, for frying
Toppings, extras and crunch (optional)

Mix together your chosen GRAIN and GLUE with the eggs, baking powder, salt, ADDITIONAL TEXTURE and SPICE, if using, to make a smooth batter – the consistency should be like a slightly runny yogurt.
   Add a teaspoon of coconut oil or butter to a pan over a medium-high heat. Spoon in a couple of tablespoons of batter and let the pancake cook for 3 minutes, until it turns golden at the edges and bubbles start to appear on the surface of the pancake. Flip and cook the other side for the same amount of time.   Top with FRUIT and/or CREAM TOPPINGS and add EXTRAS and CRUNCH, as desired.

· Blood orange
· Apples
· Berries   · Nut butter
· Quince compote   · Cacao nut butter   · Cacao nibs
· Pear   · Tahini   · Nuts
· Banana   · Orange mascarpone   · Cacao powder   · Popped grains
· Rhubarb compote   · Coconut yogurt   · Maple syrup   · Bee pollen
· Root ginger, grated   · Skyr   · Date syrup   · Seeds

FRUIT TOPPINGS   CREAM TOPPINGS   EXTRAS   CRUNCH

                         · Blue cheese   · Sriracha   · Nuts
                         · Goat's cheese   · Miso   · Popped grains
                         · Sour cream   · Olive oil (try infused · Sprouts
                         · Greek yogurt   olive oils)   · Seeds
                         · Tahini   · Poached/fried egg
                         · Nut butter

Roasted Brussels Sprouts,
Crispy Brown Rice and an Egg

Crispy rice is satisfying and adds a surprising element to any dish. The process of crisping the rice pops the grains slightly, so they have a crunchy outside and light, airy inside. It works so well with the perfectly cooked roasted Brussels sprouts, which add a touch of sweetness. The addition of a fried egg turns this into a delicious lunch, but it also makes a great side dish without the eggs.

• SERVES 4

200g long grain brown rice,
    soaked in water for 1 hour
450g Brussels sprouts, outer
    leaves discarded, quartered
6 tablespoons olive oil, plus
    extra if needed
3 garlic cloves, crushed
Juice of ½ lemon
Sea salt and black pepper
4 medium eggs
50g grated Parmesan

• Rinse and drain the rice and place in a pan with 500ml of water. Bring to the boil, then reduce the heat and cook, covered, for 20 minutes until all the water has been absorbed and the rice is fully cooked. Spread the cooked rice out over a baking tray and allow to fully dry out while you cook the Brussels sprouts.

Toss the Brussels sprouts in 2 tablespoons of the olive oil, the garlic, lemon juice, a teaspoon of sea salt and some black pepper. Tip into a roasting tray and roast for 30 minutes until the outer leaves start to colour and crisp and the sprouts are cooked the whole way through.

Once the rice has dried out, heat the remaining olive oil in a pan over a medium heat, allowing it to become really hot. Start adding the rice, half a cup at a time, and cook in the oil for 5–7 minutes, watching as it starts to crisp and turn golden. As you remove the crispy rice from the heat, you might need to add a little more olive oil. Season the crispy rice with a little sea salt.

Fry the eggs in a separate non-stick pan – you'll probably need to cook these one by one, unless you have a pan large enough to fry two at a time. Mix together the crispy rice and roasted Brussels sprouts, divide between 4 plates and top each with a fried egg and some grated Parmesan.

Brown Rice Pasta with Broccoli, Spinach and Gruyère Cheese

This recipe came to me after a particularly full day at the shop; just as I was gearing myself up for my long cycle home, I remembered that I had bought some Gruyère on a whim over the weekend. I wanted it warm, melted and in a bowl. While this would be a great option on its own, adding some fresh greens and pasta can be the perfect end to any day. It's also a breeze to make. The brown rice pasta has a particularly glutinous quality which makes it perfect for this dish, but wholewheat pasta would work too.

- SERVES 2

Sea salt and black pepper
250g brown rice penne pasta
    (you could use wholemeal
    pasta instead)
3 tablespoons olive oil
½ onion, finely chopped
220g Tenderstem broccoli,
    roughly chopped
1 garlic clove, crushed
60ml white wine
100g Gruyère cheese, grated
125ml Oat Cream (see page 234)
100g spinach
Juice of ½ lemon
Rocket leaves, to serve (optional)
Chilli flakes, to serve (optional)

- Bring a large pan of water to the boil and season generously with about a tablespoon of salt. Add the pasta and cook for 7–8 minutes – start checking it after 5 minutes so it is nice and al dente.

Meanwhile, warm the olive oil in a pan over a medium heat, add the onions and soften for 8 minutes. Add the broccoli and garlic, cooking for a further 3–4 minutes. Pour in the wine and allow it to bubble for 2 minutes before adding the Gruyère, oat cream and spinach. Cook for a minute longer until the Gruyère has melted and the spinach has wilted. Season with lemon juice and salt and pepper and remove from the heat.

Mix the sauce into the drained pasta and serve. I like to top mine with a little rocket for freshness and an extra peppery kick and a little chilli for heat.

DINNER

Chana Masala

This is serious comfort food. I first made it after a particularly chilly winter run – I didn't want to go and returned home exhausted. Cooking was the last thing I felt like doing, but this dish is so simple to make and satisfying to eat that I knew it would restore me. It's fragrant and lingers (in a good way) in the kitchen. I tend to go heavy on the chilli, especially if it's cold out. This is on the menu at the shop during the winter months and the smell definitely entices a few people in. It's delicious cold, too – the quantities here will make a perfect hot meal for two and a cold and light lunch the next day.

• SERVES 3–4

200g long grain brown rice
   or wild rice, soaked in water
   for at least 1 hour
2 tablespoons coconut oil
   or olive oil
2 teaspoons cumin seeds
1 onion, thinly sliced
3 garlic cloves, finely chopped
½ thumb-sized piece of root
   ginger, finely grated
1 red chilli, finely chopped
   (deseed if you prefer less heat)
1½ teaspoons ground coriander
1½ teaspoons garam masala
½ teaspoon ground turmeric
400g can of chopped tomatoes
2 × 400g cans of cooked
   chickpeas, drained and rinsed
Sea salt and black pepper
200g spinach
Juice of 1 lemon

TO SERVE
Bunch of coriander, leaves
   picked and chopped
Lemon wedges
4 tablespoons natural yogurt

• Rinse and drain the brown rice and transfer to a medium pan. Cover with 1 litre of water, place over a medium heat and cook for 20 minutes.

Meanwhile, warm the coconut oil in a pan over a medium heat. Once hot, add the cumin seeds and allow to toast and become fragrant for about 30 seconds. Add the onion and cook for a further 8 minutes before adding the garlic, ginger and chilli and cooking for 1 minute. Add the ground spices and stir to coat the onions. Pour in the chopped tomatoes and bring to the boil. Reduce the heat to a simmer, then add the chickpeas and a slash of water, season well and let it cook for around 10 minutes.

Stir in the spinach and, once it's wilted, squeeze in the lemon juice and take off the heat.

Pile the cooked rice into bowls and top with the chana masala. Serve each bowl topped with coriander, a lemon wedge and a tablespoon of yogurt.

Broccoli Soup with Popped Black Rice and Crispy Kale

This is one of my go-to soup recipes. Which says a lot because I don't have a particular affection for soup – I tend to miss the texture and individual tastes of different vegetables. However, this bright and delicious green bowlful changed my mind – the popped black rice gives it the bite that I'm always missing.

- SERVES 6

FOR THE SOUP
3 tablespoons olive oil
1 onion, finely chopped
4 garlic cloves, finely chopped
1 carrot, roughly chopped
2 leeks, washed and roughly
    chopped
1 teaspoon cumin seeds
1 broccoli head, roughly chopped
2 large tomatoes, roughly
    chopped
200g spinach
1 litre hot vegetable stock
½ bunch of parsley, leaves picked
    and finely chopped
Finely grated zest and juice
    of ½ unwaxed lemon
Sea salt and black pepper

FOR THE RICE AND KALE
75g black or wild rice, rinsed and
    soaked for ½ hour
100g kale, stems discarded
2 tablespoons olive oil
3 tablespoons coconut oil
Crumbled Stilton, to serve
    (optional)

- Preheat the oven to 180°C/fan 160°C/350°F/gas mark 4.

Place the black rice in a pan and cover with 500ml of water. Bring to the boil, then reduce the heat and simmer for 20 minutes until all the water has disappeared. Drain away any excess water and spread the rice out on a baking sheet to dry out.

Make the soup. Warm the olive oil in a large pan over a medium heat and fry the onion, garlic, carrot and leeks for 10 minutes until soft, adding the cumin seeds after 8 minutes. Add the broccoli, tomatoes and a big pinch of salt and cook for 4 more minutes. Add the spinach and stock and bring to the boil. Take the soup off the heat and add the parsley, lemon zest and juice and plenty of salt and pepper. Transfer the soup to a blender or blitz with a hand-held stick blender until smooth. Keep warm.

Meanwhile, massage the kale with olive oil, season then spread out on a baking tray and bake in the oven for 12–15 minutes until crisp. Keep warm.

To pop the rice, heat the coconut oil in a pan over a medium-high heat and, once hot, add the cooked black rice. Fry the rice, stirring occasionally until crisp on the outside, for about 3 minutes. Scoop it out of the pan and drain off excess oil on kitchen paper.

Divide the broccoli soup between bowls and top each one with the popped black rice, crispy kale and crumbled Stilton.

'Bread Sauce' Porridge

My dad does all the cooking at Christmas. While the rest of us sleep late or hang around in pyjamas he's grinding away and cooking everything to perfection. It's a flawless display, which is why I remember the tiniest time it went awry. One year, there weren't enough breadcrumbs set aside for the sauce – for my grandpa there are only really two essentials for Christmas lunch: large roasted whole cloves of garlic and bread sauce. Scouring the cupboards, we found some oats and decided to risk making an oaty 'bread sauce'. And it was a resounding success! Now it's a family tradition and is certainly not relegated just to Christmas. I've developed it into a warming porridge that hits the spot on any cold evening, especially with roasted veg and gravy.

- SERVES 2
  (OR 4 AS A SIDE)

500ml Oat Milk (see page 234)
1 onion, peeled and halved
6 cloves
6 black peppercorns
2 garlic cloves
Sprig of thyme
100g rolled oats, soaked in 250ml
   water for at least 30 minutes
Sea salt
Pinch of freshly grated nutmeg
Leftover roasted vegetables
   and gravy, to serve (optional)

- Place the oat milk, onion, cloves, peppercorns, garlic and thyme in a pan over a medium-low heat and warm slowly. After about 10 minutes, when everything has infused, strain the oat milk, discarding the onions and flavourings and return to the pan.

Rinse the soaked rolled oats and add them to the oat milk. Add a good pinch of salt and the grated nutmeg and cook for 3–4 minutes, stirring all the time, until it thickens to a porridge-like consistency.

Serve topped with leftover roasted vegetables and gravy, if you have some.

Egg-fried Rice with Spring Onions, Chilli and Tenderstem Broccoli

The possibilities of this dish are endless. I've used long grain rice here as I think it works the best, but you could use whole quinoa or millet. It's perfect for using up any leftover grains and there's nothing to stop you adding a combination – take this recipe as a base and add vegetables, fish, prawns or meat. I tend to turn to this when I invite friends over at the last minute for a bite to eat, as it doesn't require a big haul to the shops.

• SERVES 2

50g long grain brown rice,
    soaked in water for 1 hour
2 tablespoons sesame oil,
    plus extra if needed
4 spring onions, thinly sliced
1 red chilli, deseeded and
    thinly sliced
1 garlic clove, crushed
40g frozen peas, defrosted
220g Tenderstem broccoli
1 large egg, beaten
2 tablespoons tamari
Small bunch of coriander,
    finely chopped (optional)

• Drain the soaked rice and add it to a pan with 500ml of water. Let it cook for 20 minutes over a medium heat until all the water has disappeared and the rice is soft, but with the faintest bite. Drain away the excess water if necessary and set aside to dry out a little and cool.

Add the sesame oil, spring onions, chilli and garlic to a large frying pan or wok over a medium heat and soften for 4 minutes. Add the peas and broccoli and cook for a further minute, stirring regularly.

Now add the rice, with a little more sesame oil if necessary. Let it sit for a moment before stirring it to allow the rice to crisp up slightly. Stir and let it sit again. After about 5 minutes, move the rice and veg to the side, making a space for the egg. Add the beaten egg, stirring continuously and allowing it to scramble slightly, and then start folding it through the rest of the mixture. Remove from the heat and stir through the tamari and coriander, if using, before serving.

Aubergine Stew

I've talked about the many different ways aubergines can be used in recipes and hopefully by now you're starting to believe me. This smoky, sweet and spicy dish is perfect in all seasons – it's particularly comforting as the leaves start changing, but is also refreshing at the end of a summer's day. The rice can either be served alongside the dish or stirred in for an additional texture and flavour.

- SERVES 4

4 tablespoons olive oil,
  plus extra if needed
2 aubergines, cut into
  3–4cm cubes
Sea salt and black pepper
1 small onion, thinly sliced
3 garlic cloves, crushed with
  a little sea salt
1 teaspoon ground cumin
1 tablespoon coriander seeds
2 teaspoons sweet
  smoked paprika
1 cinnamon stick
1 red pepper, deseeded
  and cut into thin strips
400g can of chopped tomatoes
3 tablespoons red wine vinegar
3 tablespoons honey
6 dried apricots, chopped
200g long grain brown rice,
  soaked in water for at least
  1 hour
Large handful of coriander
  leaves, picked and roughly
  chopped
Large handful of mint leaves,
  picked and roughly chopped
Chopped pistachios,
  to serve

- Heat the oil in a deep pan over a medium-high heat. Once hot, season the aubergine with salt and fry until golden brown on all sides, adding a little extra oil if it needs it. Remove the aubergine from the pan and set aside.

Return the pan to the heat and reduce the temperature to low. Add the onion and cook slowly for 10 minutes until it starts to caramelise, then add the garlic, cumin, coriander seeds, paprika and cinnamon stick. Stir to combine, and then add the pepper. Cook slowly for 8 minutes until the pepper has softened, then add the chopped tomatoes. When the mixture begins to simmer add the vinegar, honey and apricots and continue cooking for 15 minutes until slightly reduced.

Meanwhile, drain the rice and transfer to a medium pan. Cover with 1 litre of water, place over a medium heat and cook for 20 minutes until tender.

Add the cooked aubergine to the tomato sauce and cook for another 8–10 minutes over a low heat. Serve the stew with the rice and a good sprinkling of coriander, mint and chopped pistachios, and perhaps a refreshing side salad of carrot and mint.

Baked Chicken with Sun-dried Tomatoes and Oat Cream

• SERVES 4

4 chicken thighs, skin on
Sea salt and black pepper
2 tablespoons olive oil, plus
    extra if needed
1 onion, thinly sliced
2 garlic cloves, crushed
250ml Oat Cream (see page 234)
10 sun-dried tomatoes,
    finely chopped
1 teaspoon dried oregano
1 teaspoon dried thyme
Large handful of basil leaves, torn
1 teaspoon chilli flakes
Finely grated zest of 1 unwaxed
    lemon and juice of ½
220ml chicken stock

Living in Dublin was my first experience of hosting dinner parties for friends and I loved it. I lived in a house with some amazing girls and they taught me this great recipe for chicken thighs that we would cook regularly for a big crowd. I've chosen to use oat cream instead of real cream, as I love the added sweetness it gives and how it thickens the sauce beautifully as it cooks.

• Preheat the oven to 220°C/fan 200°C/425°F/gas mark 7. Place the chicken thighs in a bowl and season generously with salt and pepper; leave for 10 minutes.

Warm the olive oil in an ovenproof pan over a medium-high heat and add the chicken thighs, skin side down. Cook until golden brown, about 4–5 minutes, then flip the thighs over and cook for a further 4 minutes. Remove the chicken from the pan and set aside.

Add a little more olive oil to the same pan if you need to and add the onion, allowing it to soften for about 8 minutes. Add the garlic and cook for a minute longer. Pour in the oat cream, sun-dried tomatoes, oregano, thyme, half the basil, the chilli flakes, lemon zest and stock and give the mix a good stir. Add the chicken thighs to the creamy sauce, stirring to combine and cooking over a low heat for a few minutes.

Transfer the pan to the oven and bake for 20 minutes until the chicken is lovely and golden. Remove from the oven, squeeze over the lemon juice and scatter over the remaining basil. Serve with some vegetables or a grain of your choice.

Wild Mushroom
Barley Risotto with Scallops

• SERVES 4

4 tablespoons olive oil
1 banana shallot, finely chopped
2 celery sticks, finely chopped
3 garlic cloves, finely chopped
20g dried porcini, soaked
    in 250ml boiling water for
    5 minutes
250g pearl barley
1 litre hot vegetable stock
Sea salt and black pepper
400g wild mushrooms such
    as girolles, torn in half
40g unsalted butter
Handful of parsley leaves,
    picked and finely chopped
Squeeze of lemon juice

FOR THE SCALLOPS
1 tablespoon olive oil or butter
8 large (king) scallops
8 sage leaves

I don't get many cravings but, when I'm exhausted, I need mushrooms. I can't explain it but perhaps there's a vitamin or something in them that I'm lacking as they really hit the spot. A muggy climate like ours in the UK provides the means for a healthy growth and variety of mushrooms in the autumn. They can become the standout ingredient of this dish with just a little garlic, lemon and butter. Scallops are another of my favourite ingredients: here the dark, rich mushroom risotto complements their sweet softness. Better than a sleep, if you ask me. You can easily scale this up to serve more at a dinner party, or scale down to create a special meal for two.

• Warm 3 tablespoons of the olive oil in a deep pan over a medium heat. Add the shallot, celery and 2 of the garlic cloves. Cook slowly, stirring occasionally, for 10 minutes. Scoop the porcini from the soaking water (keep the water to add later), then finely chop and stir into the vegetables. Cook for a further 3 minutes, then stir in the pearl barley and fry for 3 minutes.

Pour in the porcini soaking liquid and, once it has been absorbed, add a quarter of the stock, continuing like this for 40–45 minutes until the stock has been used up and the barley is tender. Season to taste and put to one side to rest while you prepare the mushrooms and scallops.

Warm the remaining olive oil in a frying pan over a medium-high heat and add the remaining garlic. Fry for just a moment, then stir in the wild mushrooms and cook for a few minutes until they begin to colour and wilt slightly. Stir in the butter and, once it's melted, stir in the parsley and lemon juice. Season to taste and then stir into the pearl barley.

Wipe out the frying pan and return to a medium-high heat with the olive oil. Once hot, add the scallops and cook for a minute until golden on the underside. Turn them over, add the sage leaves to the pan and cook for another minute. Remove from the heat and serve the scallops on top of the pearl barley risotto.

•——→

Smoked Haddock, Leek and Rye Tart

As the days become shorter, fish becomes even more important in Denmark and locally sourced fish is the staple on menus and in home cooking. It is also a rich source of vitamin D, of which we're deprived when there's limited sunlight. This delicious tart is great when served warm with salad or wrapped up and taken with you for lunch on a day out.

• SERVES 8–10

FOR THE PASTRY
120g rye flakes, blitzed in a food processor to a coarse flour (or use rye flour), plus extra for dusting
60g rolled oats, blitzed in a food processor to a coarse flour (or use oat flour)
60g ground almonds
1 teaspoon sea salt
1 teaspoon dill seeds (optional)
2 medium eggs
250g unsalted butter, cut into cubes

FOR THE PICKLED ONION
1 red onion, thinly sliced
5 black peppercorns
½ teaspoon honey
½ teaspoon sea salt
200ml apple cider vinegar

FOR THE FILLING
250ml whole milk or Oat Milk (see page 234)
150ml double cream
2 large leeks, washed and finely sliced
2 bay leaves
250g smoked haddock
5 medium eggs
Small handful of dill, finely chopped
Small handful of parsley leaves, picked and finely chopped
Sea salt and black pepper

• First make the pastry. Tip all the dry ingredients into a large bowl and stir to combine. Add the water, eggs and butter and stir with a round-bladed knife to form a dough. Form into a ball, then wrap in cling film and chill in the fridge for 20–25 minutes.

Meanwhile, make the pickled onion. Pour hot water from the kettle over the sliced onion to blanch it, then drain and add to a small bowl with the peppercorns. In a small pan, warm the honey, salt and vinegar over a low heat until the salt has dissolved, then pour over the onions. Leave to pickle for about 20 minutes.

Roll the dough out on a lightly floured surface to a circle about 5mm thick, then use to line a 25cm loose-bottomed tart tin, pushing it into the edges and leaving a little pastry hanging over the edge. Prick the base a couple of times with a fork, then place in the freezer for 15 minutes to firm up. Preheat the oven to 180°C/fan 160°C/350°F/gas mark 4.

Remove the lined tin from the freezer and cover with baking paper and baking beans. Bake blind for 10–12 minutes, removing the paper and beans after 5 minutes. Remove from the oven when golden and firm to the touch, then leave to cool.

Meanwhile, prepare the filling. Place the milk, cream, leeks and bay leaves in a wide, flat pan and gently bring to the boil. Reduce the heat to a simmer, then add the fish and cook for 5 minutes until just cooked. Remove from the heat and leave the fish to cool in the milk for 10 minutes. Remove the fish from the milk, discarding the skin, and break into flakes. Discard the bay leaves.

Whisk the eggs, then add the milk (and leeks), herbs and plenty of seasoning. Gently fold in the flaked fish, then pour into the cooled pastry case. Bake in the oven for 30–40 minutes, or until golden in colour and set in the middle. Serve with the pickled onions.

Coconut and Butternut Squash Curry with Black Sticky Rice

Butternut squash is a wonderful winter vegetable – delicious when simply roasted or puréed or made into a curry, as in this recipe, where it adds a lovely sweetness to the coconut and fragrant spices. You needn't limit yourself to just one kind – try using different types such as the striped Delicata, knobbly Hubbard or Japanese Kabocha squash for slightly different textures and sweetness.

- **SERVES 4**

FOR THE RICE
100g Chinese black sticky rice, soaked in water for at least 1 hour
1 teaspoon ground cumin
1 teaspoon sea salt

FOR THE CURRY
2 tablespoons coconut or olive oil
2 onions, finely chopped
Sea salt and black pepper
1 garlic clove, finely chopped
Thumb-sized piece of root ginger, finely chopped
1–2 red chillies, sliced (deseed if you prefer less heat)
1 heaped teaspoon ground turmeric
1 teaspoon ground coriander
1 medium butternut squash, peeled, deseeded and sliced into 3cm cubes
350ml hot vegetable stock
400ml can of coconut milk
1 tablespoon fish sauce
1 teaspoon honey
Finely grated zest and juice of 1 unwaxed lime

TO SERVE
Handful of coriander leaves, picked and roughly chopped
1 lime, quartered

- Drain the black rice and rinse well under cold water. Place in a pan, add 500ml of water and bring to the boil, then reduce the heat, cover and simmer for 30–40 minutes until the liquid has been absorbed and the rice is tender and a little chewy.

Meanwhile, start the curry by heating the oil in a large, deep pan. Add the onions and a good pinch of salt and cook for 8–10 minutes, or until softened, but not coloured.

Reduce the heat to low and add the garlic, ginger, chillies and spices to the pan. Cook for a minute until the spices start to smell fragrant, then stir in the squash. The spices will dry out the contents of the pan slightly, but don't be tempted to add more oil. Allow to cook for a minute longer, then increase the heat to medium and add half the stock and half the coconut milk. As soon as this starts bubbling, add the remaining stock and coconut milk, the fish sauce, honey and lime zest and juice. Season to taste, then reduce the heat to low again and leave to simmer for 10–15 minutes until the squash is tender.

Once the rice is cooked, stir in the cumin and salt and divide between 4 serving bowls. Ladle the coconut squash curry on top and serve scattered with fresh coriander and a lime wedge to squeeze over.

Rye Berries and Miso Butternut with Broad Bean Smash and Marinated Kale

Rye is more commonly known in the form of flour or flaked grain but rye berries (whole rye grains) are chewy and full of flavour. You can find them from online suppliers (or simply substitute for pearled spelt or barley). Rye does ferment easily, so if you leave them to soak too long you might find you've made a fermented rye berry salad, a slightly more tangy, and some might argue, fuller flavoured dish. For this recipe, I wanted the rye to complement the earthiness of the baked sweet squash. Contrasting this is the soft, fresh broad bean smash and lightly marinated kale. Getting each component on a fork makes for some very satisfying mouthfuls.

- SERVES 4

100g rye berries (or pearled spelt
  or barley), soaked in water for at
  least 1 hour
Rocket, to serve

FOR THE MISO BUTTERNUT
2 tablespoons sesame oil
2 tablespoons organic fermented
  brown rice miso paste
2 tablespoons mirin
1 tablespoon honey
1 teaspoon smooth hot mustard
squeeze of lemon juice
1 tablespoon tamari
1 small butternut squash (about 700g),
  unpeeled, halved, deseeded
  and sliced into 1cm half moons
Sea salt and black pepper

FOR THE MARINATED KALE
1 tablespoon apple cider vinegar
1 tablespoon honey
1 tablespoon extra-virgin olive oil
75g kale (purple or green),
  stems discarded

FOR THE BROAD BEAN SMASH
100g frozen peas
100g frozen broad beans
2 large handfuls of mint leaves
3 tablespoons extra-virgin olive oil
Finely grated zest and juice
  of ½ unwaxed lemon

- Preheat the oven to 200°C/fan 180°C/400°F/gas mark 6 and line a baking tray with baking paper.

Drain and rinse the rye berries, then place in a pan with 500ml of water and bring to the boil. Reduce the heat to a simmer, cover and cook for 20–30 minutes until the berries are tender and most of the water has disappeared.

Meanwhile, for the miso butternut, mix the wet ingredients together in a large bowl, add the squash slices and mix so that the squash is completely coated. Arrange the slices on the lined baking tray, season lightly and cook in the oven for 30 minutes, turning occasionally until completely tender and dark brown. The miso paste will darken quite quickly, so cover with a layer of baking paper if you're worried about it burning.

While the squash is in the oven pour the apple cider vinegar, honey and olive oil into a bowl, season and add the kale. Rub the kale in the marinade with your hands until it starts to soften, then put to one side.

●———→

●———→

Next make the broad bean smash. Place the frozen peas and
beans in a pan, cover with boiling water and place over a high
heat. As soon as it returns to the boil, take off the heat and drain.
Pop the beans, peas, mint, olive oil and lemon zest and juice into
a food processor or blender and pulse until you have
a coarse smash. Taste and adjust the seasoning.

Whisk together all the ingredients for the dressing, seasoning well.
Once the rye berries and butternut are cooked, mix them together
in a large bowl and add the marinated kale and dressing. Season
with salt and pepper and then divide between 4 plates. Top each
with a good dollop of broad bean smash and some rocket.

FOR THE DRESSING
3 tablespoons extra-virgin olive oil
2 tablespoons apple cider vinegar
½ teaspoon English mustard
½ teaspoon honey
½ garlic clove, crushed with a little
   sea salt

Spicy Sweet Potato and Amaranth with Ginger Crème Fraîche

I had my wisdom teeth removed last year and it was during this time that I looked for the softest, most yielding, tasty foods I could find. Sweet potato and delicate amaranth proved to be a godsend. I wasn't convinced I was the most discerning critic at the time, so when I served some leftovers to my brothers and they hoovered it up, I was pleasantly surprised. It's the definition of comfort food: sweet, nourishing and warming with a refreshing and nutty flavour from the amaranth. The heat from the chilli adds a nice depth and prevents it from falling into baby food territory. We serve this dish in the shop in winter with Marinated Kale – if you'd like to do the same, see the recipe on page 108 to turn this into a more substantial main dish.

SERVES 2–3

50g whole amaranth, soaked
  in water for 1 hour
375ml hot vegetable stock
800g sweet potatoes, peeled
  and cubed
Sea salt and black pepper
1 teaspoon ground coriander
1 red chilli, thickly sliced
  (deseed if you prefer less heat)
Juice of ½ lemon
1 tablespoon olive oil
1 × quantity Marinated Kale
  (optional, see page 108)
Small handful of coriander leaves,
  picked and roughly torn,
  to serve

FOR THE GINGER CRÈME FRAÎCHE
½ thumb-sized piece of root
  ginger, finely grated
Juice of 1 lime
1 teaspoon extra-virgin olive oil
4 tablespoons crème fraîche

- Rinse and drain the soaked amaranth and transfer to a medium pan. Pour over the stock and bring to the boil. Reduce the heat and cook over a medium heat for 20 minutes until all the stock has been absorbed. Remove from the heat and leave to stand with the lid on.

Meanwhile place the sweet potatoes in a pan of cold water with 1 teaspoon of salt and bring to the boil. Cook for 10 minutes, or until soft enough to mash.

While the amaranth and potatoes cook, make the ginger crème fraîche by mixing all the ingredients together in a bowl until well combined, seasoning to taste.

Once the potatoes are cooked, pop them into a food processor or blender and add the ground coriander, chilli, lemon juice, olive oil and a little black pepper. Blitz to a smooth purée, then stir in the cooked amaranth and taste and adjust the seasoning.

Pour the sweet potato and amaranth into 2 or 3 bowls and top with the Marinated Kale, if using, the ginger crème fraîche and a good sprinkling of coriander.

Autumn Salad with Roasted Buckwheat, Walnuts and Labneh

Autumn is my favourite season; I'm known for being endlessly distracted by the light, colours and the produce. In my little garden I can watch the pears on the tree grow plump and hot pink chard stems sprouting up. The air becomes just cool enough to hang the labneh on an outside door handle, to let it strain. You can let it drip into a bowl while you get started on pickling the beetroot and preparing the salad. Buckwheat adds a unique earthy crunch to the salad and lends a smokiness when it's all combined.

- **SERVES 4**

FOR THE LABNEH
200g Greek-style yogurt
200g natural yogurt
Pinch of sea salt

FOR THE BEETROOT PICKLE
1 beetroot, thinly sliced with a mandoline
1 golden beetroot, thinly sliced with a mandoline
60ml apple cider vinegar
2 tablespoons honey
Pinch of sea salt
¼ teaspoon dill seeds
¼ teaspoon yellow mustard seeds

FOR THE SALAD
100g buckwheat groats, soaked in water for 30 minutes
4 tablespoons olive oil
200g rainbow chard, stems removed, washed and torn
1 pear, cored and thinly sliced
1 cucumber, sliced into 8cm sticks
Bunch of radishes, washed and halved
Juice of 1 lemon
½ garlic clove, crushed with a little sea salt
Sea salt and black pepper
30g walnuts, roughly chopped, to serve (optional)

- Make the labneh first, either the night before or over the course of an afternoon. Combine the yogurts and salt in a bowl, then transfer to a sheet of muslin or a clean tea towel, pull up the sides, tie up the top with an elastic band or string and suspend over a bowl to let the liquids drain out for at least 6 hours, or overnight if possible.

Meanwhile place all the ingredients for the beetroot pickle in a bowl with 60ml/4 tablespoons of water. Leave to pickle in the fridge for several hours or overnight.

The following day, rinse the soaked buckwheat under running hot water for 2 minutes, then drain and pat dry with kitchen paper. Add 1 tablespoon of the oil to a frying pan and place over a medium-low heat. Add the buckwheat and toast for 2 minutes until golden, stirring continuously so it doesn't burn.

Mix the rainbow chard, pear, cucumber, pickled beetroot, radishes, remaining olive oil, lemon juice and garlic together and season well with sea salt and pepper. Stir in half the toasted buckwheat.

Divide between 4 plates and top with a good dollop or so of labneh, a sprinkle of the remaining buckwheat and walnuts, if using.

Roasted Turmeric Cauliflower with Quinoa, Samphire and Dukkah

Roasting is one of my favourite ways to enjoy cauliflower. I like how the branches of the core soften as the outer stems start to crisp and soak up the garlic, lemon and turmeric dressing. Quinoa pairs particularly well with citrus flavours and can really emphasise its freshness. Combined with the saltiness of the samphire, this is a seriously satisfying dish that has people asking for the recipe over and over again.

- SERVES 2

3 tablespoons olive oil
1 teaspoon ground turmeric
Juice of 1 lemon
1 red chilli, deseeded and thinly
  sliced, plus ½ chopped red
  chilli, to serve
Sea salt and black pepper
1 small cauliflower
100g whole quinoa, rinsed
  well and soaked in water
  for at least 30 minutes
150g samphire
Extra-virgin olive oil, to serve

FOR THE DUKKAH SPRINKLE
40g flaked almonds
25g sesame seeds
½ tablespoon cumin seeds
½ teaspoon sea salt
½ teaspoon dried thyme

- Preheat the oven to 200°C/fan 180°C/400°F/gas mark 6.

Combine the oil, turmeric, lemon juice and chilli in a large bowl and season well. Cut the cauliflower in half lengthways, then add to the bowl and rub in the lemony oil. Place on a baking tray, then roast for 30 minutes until just tender, turning it over halfway through the cooking time.

While the cauliflower is in the oven, rinse and drain the quinoa and place in a pan with 250ml of water. Bring to the boil, then reduce the heat and simmer vigorously for 15–20 minutes until the quinoa is just cooked and all the water has been absorbed. Remove from the heat, cover and leave to stand for a few minutes.

Bring 2cm of water to the boil in a pan and lightly steam the samphire for 1–2 minutes; drain and set aside.

Meanwhile, make the dukkah sprinkle by combining all the ingredients in a food processor. Blitz a couple of times until you have a coarse powder (you want it to be quite textured).

To assemble the dish, place the roasted cauliflower halves on 2 plates or bowls. Stir the steamed samphire through the quinoa, season to taste (bearing in mind that both the samphire and dukkah are quite salty), then spoon the mix over the cauliflower. Sprinkle everything with plenty of dukkah and add a little red chilli and a good drizzle of olive oil to serve. (You'll have lots of dukkah left over – just store in an airtight container and use as a spicy seasoning.)

Roasted Sesame Veg
with Pearl Barley
and Cinnamon Dressing

• SERVES 4

FOR THE ROASTED VEG
4 carrots, quartered lengthways
4 parsnips, quartered lengthways
2 red onions, quartered
  lengthways
3 tablespoons olive oil
Sea salt and black pepper

FOR THE PEARL BARLEY
2 tablespoons olive oil
1 white onion, thinly sliced
1 garlic clove, finely chopped
200g pearl barley, soaked
  in water for 1 hour
1 litre hot vegetable stock

FOR THE CINNAMON DRESSING
6 tablespoons olive oil
1 garlic clove, thinly sliced
1 tablespoon honey
1 teaspoon ground cinnamon
1 teaspoon sesame seeds
Juice of 2 limes

It's hard to play favourites with grains as often what I'm craving is dependent on the season, time of day or my mood. But barley is the most comforting to me. It swells up when cooked and can become creamy in consistency without being mushy. For the roasted vegetables aubergine and squash would work well, too, so use whatever is fresh, to hand or grabs your attention. You might think adding cinnamon to the mix would make it overly sweet, but paired with the earthy veg and sesame it becomes something far more complex. I'd recommend cooking too much on a cold night and sharing with friends and family for a *hygge*-filled evening.

• Preheat the oven to 200°C/fan 180°C/400°F/gas mark 6. Spread the veg over a baking tray, drizzle over the olive oil and season well with salt and pepper. Toss with your hands so everything is nicely coated, then roast for 35–45 minutes, shaking the tray occasionally, until the veg is soft and beginning to turn golden at the edges.

Meanwhile cook the barley: add the olive oil to a pan over a medium heat and cook the onion for 10 minutes until softened. Add the garlic and cook for a minute longer. Rinse and drain the barley and stir it into the onions before adding the stock. Bring to the boil and then reduce the heat to medium and cook for 30–40 minutes, or until the barley is tender but still with some bite.

Make the cinnamon dressing: add 1 tablespoon of the olive oil to a medium pan and cook the garlic gently for a couple of minutes. Stir in the honey, cinnamon, the remaining olive oil, sesame seeds, lime juice and 2 tablespoons of water and cook for a few minutes longer, stirring until it all comes together.

Five minutes before the roasted veg are ready, remove from the oven and pour half of the cinnamon sauce over them, making sure they are evenly coated. Return to the oven for 5 minutes to caramelise.

Pile the barley into 4 bowls and top with the roasted veg and remaining cinnamon dressing. Season well with salt and pepper before serving.

How to Make
Leftover Grain Patties

This recipe is a super way to use up leftover cooked grains and salads and to make satisfying dishes with endless possibilities. Here is one of my favourites, but play with different ingredients, sweet or savoury, to find yours.

- **MAKES 5 SMALL PATTIES**

80g cooked grains
   (any type)
20g rolled oats, blitzed
   in a food processor
   to a coarse flour
   (or use oat flour)
1 medium egg, beaten
50g salty cheese, such
   as feta or halloumi,
   chopped (optional)
30g chard, kale
   or spinach, stems
   discarded, torn
½ garlic clove, crushed
Squeeze of lemon juice
Sea salt and
   black pepper
Olive oil, for frying

- Mix all the ingredients except the oil together in a bowl until well combined and press into a single ball. Cover with cling film and chill in the fridge for 20 minutes.

Remove the mixture from the fridge and shape into little patties, about 10cm in diameter.

Warm a splash of olive oil in frying pan over a medium heat. Pop the patties in the pan and fry for 3 minutes on each side until golden. Serve with salad, herbs and anything else that takes your fancy.

TO SERVE   Choose any of the following:

salad leaves
fresh herbs
hard-boiled eggs
harissa paste
toasted nuts   sliced fennel
tahini   apple
                          micro sprouts
                          pickles
                          roasted veg
                          Garlic Yogurt (see page 78)

How to Make
Crisped Grains

Crisping up grains, particularly any that you might have left over, is a great way of transforming a dish. Try any combination: add them to a bowl of lightly steamed fresh greens with lemon and olive oil, some slow-roasted vegetables, a poached egg, spring onions and edamame beans, carrot salad...

- SERVES 2

5 tablespoons coconut
  or olive oil
100g cooked, cooled
  and dried out grains

- Heat the oil in a pan over a medium-high heat until shiny on the surface, then add the cooked grains and fry, stirring occasionally, for 4 minutes until crisp and golden brown.

The beauty here is that you can then mix these deliciously nutty and crispy grains with anything you like. Don't hold back.

TO SERVE Choose any of the following:

poached egg
avocado
cucumber
hummus
Marinated Kale (see page 108)
sweet peppers   seeds
steak   coconut
pickles   courgette
spring onions   slow-roasted tomatoes
sprouted lentils
beetroot

peanuts
coleslaw
green beans
sumac
sweet potato
miso aubergine

Black Sticky Rice with Oyster Mushrooms

• SERVES 2

150g Chinese black sticky
  rice, soaked in water for
  at least 1 hour
2 tablespoons sesame oil
Thumb-sized piece of
  root ginger, finely chopped
4 spring onions, thinly sliced
2 red chillies, thinly sliced
  (deseed if you prefer less heat)
200g oyster mushrooms, torn
  into quarters
1 tablespoon Chinese rice wine
2 tablespoons tamari, or soy
  sauce, plus extra if needed
1 teaspoon honey
Handful of coriander leaves,
  picked, to serve

FOR THE DRESSING
2 tablespoons rice wine vinegar
1 tablespoon tamari or soy sauce
½ teaspoon honey

Big, juicy oyster mushrooms are amazing and a dream
to prep – just rinse away any of the dirt or grit and you're
good to go. They hold their texture when cooked and are
nature's sponge, soaking up any juices that they're cooked
with. The black sticky rice is a great counterpart and the
acidic dressing brings a lightness to counterbalance
the starch. If you're feeling ambitious make some peanut
butter with chilli sauce to stir in (see page 240); crushed
roasted peanuts work really well too. The best place
to find Chinese black sticky rice is in Asian supermarkets.

• Drain the black rice, then rinse well under cold water. Place in
a pan, cover with 750ml of water and bring to the boil. Reduce
the heat, cover and simmer for 40 minutes, stirring regularly so
that the rice doesn't catch on the bottom of the pan, until the
rice is just tender and the water has been absorbed.

Meanwhile make the dressing by shaking the ingredients together
in a jar with a tight-fitting lid, or whisking in a bowl.

Once the rice is cooked, heat the sesame oil in a wok or large
frying pan over a medium-high heat, add the ginger, spring onions
and chillies and allow it to cook through for a minute or so until
the spring onions are softened. Add the mushrooms and cook for
about 8 minutes. Add the rice wine and cook for 1 minute longer.

Stir the rice wine, tamari and honey into the rice. Adjust for
seasoning, adding more tamari (or soy sauce) if needed.

Transfer to 2 plates, then spoon over the dressing and sprinkle
with the coriander leaves before serving.

Spelt with Parsley-almond Pesto, Cherry Tomatoes and Parmesan

I was so excited to move to my new house last year – what sold it for me was the most beautiful, big garden. When I first viewed the house, I remember getting excited about the produce growing, both a little wild and contained, from young green tomatoes to sage, dill and a handful of strawberries. My first night in the house was a warm July evening and we decided to have a barbecue. I wanted to make something simple and delicious to accompany some of our other summer evening dishes – oysters, salad, roasted vegetables and burgers. I had spotted the large bunch of parsley in the herb patch and decided to make this light, refreshing dish.

• SERVES 4

FOR THE SPELT
200g pearled spelt, soaked
   in water for at least 1 hour
2 tablespoons olive oil
1 onion, finely chopped
1 garlic clove, crushed
250g cherry tomatoes, halved
150g rocket
50g shaved Parmesan

FOR THE PESTO
75g flaked almonds
50g parsley
1 garlic clove, crushed
100ml extra-virgin olive oil
Juice of 1 lemon
½ teaspoon of salt
Freshly ground black pepper

• Start by making the spelt. Add 1 litre of water to a medium pan and bring to the boil. Add the drained spelt and reduce the heat so the water is at a gentle rolling boil. Cook for 20 minutes until tender.

Add the olive oil to a pan over a medium heat. Add the onion and let it cook until softened, about 8 minutes, then add the garlic and cook for a minute longer. Remove from the heat and stir in the tomatoes.

To make the pesto, place all the ingredients in a food processor or blender and pulse briefly (about 6 times) for a more textured pesto, or blend at high speed for a minute or so for a smoother pesto.

Drain the cooked spelt and allow to cool slightly. Mix with the onion and tomatoes in a bowl and add stir in a good helping of the pesto – about 8 tablespoons (any leftover pesto can be stored in the fridge in an airtight jar for up to 5 days). Season with salt and pepper and serve with the rocket and shaved Parmesan.

Tomato Coconut Rice
with Halloumi and Avocado

- SERVES 6

FOR THE TOMATO COCONUT RICE
250ml short grain brown rice,
   soaked in water for at least
   1 hour
1 litre vegetable stock
2 tablespoons olive oil
2 onions, chopped
2 teaspoons ground cumin
2 red chillies, finely chopped
   (deseed if you prefer less heat)
8 large tomatoes, chopped
Sea salt and black pepper
400ml can of coconut milk

TO SERVE
1 tablespoon olive oil
2 × 250g packets of halloumi,
   cut into 1cm slices
2 avocados, halved, pitted
   and sliced
3 tablespoons roasted
   almonds, chopped
Few handfuls of alfalfa sprouts

This dish has a special place in my heart because it was the first ever savoury porridge that we put on the shop's menu and it was an instant classic. We took it off with the change of season, but still get endless requests and can't wait to get it back on the menu. Cook the tomatoes slowly so that they break down and become incredibly soft and sweet. The key to this dish is the quality of the toppings; find the plumpest avocado, the best halloumi and roasted almonds, and don't hold back.

- Drain and rinse the rice, then transfer to a pan along with the stock and place over a medium heat. Bring to the boil, then reduce the heat, cover and simmer for 30–40 minutes until tender and the water has been absorbed.

Meanwhile, warm the olive oil in a pan over a medium heat. Add the onions and cook for 10 minutes until soft, then stir in the cumin and chillies and cook for a further minute before adding the chopped tomatoes and some seasoning. Bring to the boil, then reduce the heat right down and simmer for 20 minutes until thickened.

Pour in the coconut milk and cooked rice and cook for a further 3 minutes. Season to taste, then keep warm while you cook the halloumi.

Heat the olive oil in a frying pan over a medium-high heat and, once hot, fry the halloumi on both sides until golden and completely soft. Transfer the tomato coconut rice to bowls, then top each with the halloumi, sliced avocado, almonds and alfalfa sprouts.

Courgette, Almond and Parmesan Salad with Toasted Buckwheat

This is just the thing when you're craving something light, refreshing and delicious – I love serving this salad as a contrast to barbecued food. Seasoning the courgette a little will draw out the water and soften it – if you decide to do this, be sure to drain the courgette thoroughly before mixing it with the rest of the ingredients.

- **SERVES 2**

50g buckwheat groats, soaked
   in water for at least 30 minutes
1 tablespoon coconut oil
300g courgettes, peeled
   into ribbons or noodled
   with a spiralizer
Sea salt and black pepper
40g flaked almonds
Juice of ½ lemon
50g shaved Parmesan
2 tablespoons extra-virgin
   olive oil
Good handful of basil leaves

- Rinse and drain the buckwheat and pat dry with kitchen paper. Melt the coconut oil in a small pan over a medium heat and once hot, add the buckwheat and toast for 2 minutes until golden, stirring continuously so it doesn't burn.

Place the courgettes in a sieve over a bowl and evenly sprinkle over 1 teaspoon of sea salt. Set aside for 5 minutes to draw out the water.

Meanwhile, toast the almonds in a dry frying pan over a medium heat, shaking the pan continuously until the almonds turn golden. Set to one side.

Squeeze out as much moisture as possible from the courgettes and transfer to a mixing bowl. Add the lemon juice, Parmesan, extra-virgin olive oil and a good crack of black pepper. When you're ready to serve, tear in the basil leaves and toss in the almonds and toasted buckwheat. Taste and adjust the seasoning before serving.

Beef and Barley Stew

• SERVES 6

2 tablespoons olive oil
Sea salt and black pepper
1kg braising steak, cut into
  3cm chunks
2 onions, finely chopped
1 garlic clove, finely chopped
3 bay leaves
3 parsnips, roughly chopped
3 carrots, roughly chopped
500ml hot beef stock
30g tomato purée
1 tablespoon red wine vinegar
100g pearl barley, soaked in
  water for at least 1 hour
Handful of parsley leaves, picked
  and chopped

I've come to realise that the point of dragging yourself out for a long winter walk when there are sparse hours of daylight is just so you can settle in on a dark night afterwards with a steaming bowl of food and feel like you've earned it. Don't get me wrong, I love a muddy, rainy walk – there's pleasure in the moment – but the reward at the end of it makes it even more appealing. You can make this before you set off, knowing the longer you're out the richer and more luscious and soft the meat will become. Not only that but it will keep for a good 5 days and continue to develop in flavour.

• Heat the olive oil in a large pan over a medium-high heat. Once hot, season the beef and brown on all sides, in batches if necessary. Remove from the pan and set aside.

Add the onions, garlic, bay leaves, parsnip, carrots and a pinch of salt to the pan. Reduce the heat to low and allow to soften for 8 minutes, stirring occasionally.

Return the beef to the pan along with the stock, tomato purée and vinegar, then season generously with salt and pepper. Reduce the heat and leave the stew to simmer away gently for 2½ hours.

Rinse and drain the barley then stir it into the stew for the final 40 minutes of cooking. Season with salt and pepper to taste and sprinkle over the parsley. Serve with a good slice of fresh bread.

Brown Rice Indonesian Chicken Porridge

My incredibly talented friend Tanita taught me this recipe after she spent some time in Indonesia. There is nothing more enjoyable than being taught a recipe by a friend – I find the story of where and how a dish was first learnt completely captivating, and it was exactly so with this. It is a traditional savoury porridge from Indonesia, but with a texture similar to risotto. The combination of cloves, bay, galangal and chilli warms the insides and together make an incredibly unique dish. Galangal is a member of the ginger family, but is ginger's very subtle cousin. You can find galangal in most Asian supermarkets and from many online suppliers.

- SERVES 4

FOR THE PORRIDGE

250g short grain brown rice, soaked in water for 1 hour, then drained
1.5 litres chicken stock
2 thumb-sized pieces of galangal (or use 1 piece of root ginger)
4 cloves
3 bay leaves
Pinch of sea salt
1 tablespoon coconut oil
Good pinch of white pepper

TO SERVE

1 tablespoon sesame seeds, toasted
2 tablespoons unsalted peanuts
Olive oil, for frying
200g cooked chicken, shredded
2 spring onions, thinly sliced
1 small bird's eye chilli, thinly sliced (deseed if you prefer less heat)
2 large handfuls of spinach
Handful of coriander leaves, picked and roughly chopped
Kecap manis (Indonesian sweet soy sauce) or regular soy sauce

- Place all the porridge ingredients, except the coconut oil and white pepper, in a pan and bring to the boil. Reduce the heat and simmer for 30–40 minutes, topping up with a little water if it looks like it needs it.

While the porridge cooks prepare the toppings. Toast the sesame seeds in a dry frying pan over a medium heat for 2–3 minutes, stirring continuously to stop them catching. Do the same with the peanuts to toast them too, giving them a lovely crunch and depth of flavour. Be careful not to burn them. Once the peanuts have cooled, lightly crush them with a mortar and pestle.

In the same pan, warm a little olive oil and add the shredded chicken to crisp up.

When the porridge is cooked, remove the bay leaves and galangal (or ginger), stir in the coconut oil and white pepper and taste and adjust the seasoning. Pour into bowls and top with the spring onions, chilli, spinach, chicken, peanuts, sesame seeds, coriander and kecap manis (or soy sauce) to serve.

Peppers Stuffed with Fennel Sausage and Rice

This recipe is a play on the flavours of a traditional Italian sausage, combining fennel, chilli and garlic. Mirasol red peppers add a lovely sweetness and the whole dish comes together as it bakes in the oven. For me, the best thing about this recipe is the rice, soaking up all the delicious flavours of the sausage, fennel and pepper and crisping up in the oven to add a wonderful texture.

• SERVES 4

100g long grain brown rice, soaked in water for 1 hour
Sea salt and black pepper
2 tablespoons olive oil, plus extra to drizzle
1 onion, thinly sliced
1 fennel bulb, trimmed and thinly sliced
½ teaspoon fennel seeds
2 sage leaves, sliced
400g good-quality pork sausages, casings removed
Pinch of chilli flakes
1 tablespoon sherry or white wine
4 long sweet red peppers (such as Mirasol), halved and deseeded
Handful of parsley leaves, finely chopped, to garnish

• Drain and rinse the rice and place in a pan with 500ml of boiling water and ½ teaspoon sea salt. Cook over a medium heat until completely tender, about 20 minutes, then drain.

Meanwhile, preheat the oven to 180°C/fan 160°C/350°F/gas mark 4 and line a roasting tray with baking paper.

Heat the olive oil in a pan over a medium heat. Add the onion, fennel, fennel seeds and sage along with a good pinch of salt. Fry for 8 minutes until softened, then increase the heat a little and crumble in the sausagemeat and chilli. Fry for another 3 minutes until the sausage begins to colour, then add the sherry or wine, wait a moment for it to bubble away, then stir in the cooked and drained rice. Remove from the heat, season to taste and then spoon into the pepper halves.

Place the filled peppers in the roasting tray. Bake in the oven for 30 minutes until soft and the edges are starting to crisp. Add a good sprinkling of parsley and serve with a green salad or other vegetables.

Red Rice Salad with Prawns and Mango Salsa

This reminds me of summers gone by: fresh delicious prawns, juicy ripe mangoes and the smell of the coals slowly burning on the barbecue. Sit outside to prepare the food, enjoy the sun and get ready for the feast ahead. I adore the red rice in this recipe – it keeps a great texture and is incredibly nutty in flavour. The juices from the cooked prawns and salsa will slowly trickle through and are captured by the grains below. Serve with a refreshing mint and citrus ice-cold drink for the ultimate in summer satisfaction.

- SERVES 4

FOR THE RICE SALAD

150g red rice (or use brown
  or wild rice), soaked in water
  for 30 minutes
Sea salt and black pepper
Bunch of coriander, leaves picked
  and chopped
Bunch of mint, leaves chopped
2 tablespoons olive oil
Juice of 1 lime
100g cashew nuts, toasted and
  roughly chopped

FOR THE PRAWNS

16 raw peeled king prawns
1 garlic clove, finely chopped
1 red chilli, finely chopped
  (deseed if you prefer less heat)
1 tablespoon olive oil

FOR THE SALSA

1 ripe mango, peeled, stoned
  and cut into cubes
1 avocado, peeled, pitted and
  cut into cubes
1 large tomato, cut into cubes
Large handful of coriander
  leaves, picked and chopped
Juice of ½ lime
Sea salt and black pepper

- Drain and rinse the rice, then transfer to a pan with 750ml of water and a teaspoon of salt. Bring to the boil and cook for 30–40 minutes, or until tender and all or most of the water has been absorbed.

While the rice cooks, marinate the prawns by placing them in a bowl with the garlic, chilli and oil, rubbing the marinade into them well.

Prepare the salsa by combining all the ingredients in a bowl; season to taste with salt and pepper.

Drain the rice if it needs it, then transfer to a bowl along with the remaining salad ingredients. Season well and mix together with your hands. Put to one side while you cook the prawns.

Heat up your grill, griddle pan or barbecue to high and, once hot, grill the prawns on both sides until they turn from blue to deep orange. Transfer the rice salad to 4 plates, then top each serving with 4 pink prawns and a big spoonful of the salsa.

Trout with Freekeh, Rainbow Chard and Toasted Pine Nuts

• SERVES 2

50g freekeh, soaked in water
   for at least 1 hour
Sea salt and black pepper
30g toasted pine nuts
1 tablespoon white wine vinegar
Olive oil
1 banana shallot, thinly sliced
1 garlic clove, thinly sliced
200g rainbow chard, washed
   and stalks and leaves
   roughly chopped
1 bay leaf
1 lemon
2 × 100g rainbow trout fillets
Handful of parsley leaves,
   finely chopped

The beautiful colours of rainbow chard start to fill odd corners of our garden in the late summer and autumn. It is another delicious, dark-hued leaf that only needs the simplest of seasoning for its unique taste and texture to come through. Paired with fresh flaky trout and freekeh, with its natural malt-like tone, this dish works best in a bowl, all mixed together. Chard is best cooked and eaten the day you buy it, before it has a chance to wilt.

• Rinse and drain the freekeh, then transfer to a pan, add 500ml of water and a pinch of salt and cook over a medium heat for 20 minutes. Once cooked, drain, then stir in the pine nuts, vinegar and a splash of olive oil, season and put to one side.

In a large pan over a medium heat, warm up a splash of olive oil and fry the shallot and the garlic until soft, about 5 minutes. Stir in the chard, add 1 tablespoon of water and the bay leaf, then cover and leave to wilt for a couple of minutes, being careful not to overcook it. Once wilted, remove from the heat and season with salt and pepper and the juice of half the lemon.

Place a large frying pan over a medium-high heat and add a splash of oil. Once nice and hot, season the trout fillets and place skin-side down in the pan. Cook for 3–4 minutes, before turning over and cooking for another minute or so – take care as it can quickly overcook.

Pile the freekeh and rainbow chard on to 2 plates and top each with a trout fillet. Scatter with the chopped parsley and serve with the remaining lemon half, cut into wedges.

Smoked Salmon
on Baked Millet Slices

Beetroot and smoked salmon have long been a great match and this recipe is no exception. The new player in this dish is millet, an equally good partner to beetroot. Together, the beetroot baked through with the millet makes a soft, crumpet-like pillow for the salmon and becomes a wonderfully fresh yet filling dish.

- SERVES 4

A little flavourless oil
500g cooked beetroot
100g whole millet, rinsed
    well and soaked in water
    for at least 1 hour
Finely grated zest of
    ½ unwaxed lemon
1 teaspoon dill seeds
2 medium eggs, beaten
Sea salt and black pepper

TO SERVE
200g smoked salmon
4 tablespoons crème fraîche
Small handful of dill, fronds torn
Lemon wedges

- Preheat the oven to 180°C/fan 160°C/350°F/gas mark 4 and oil and line a baking tray with baking paper.

Place the beetroot in a food processor or blender and whizz to a smooth purée. Tip into a bowl. Rinse and drain the millet and add to the beetroot with 500ml of water, the lemon zest, dill seeds and beaten eggs; stir to combine. Season generously with salt and pepper and then pour the mixture into the lined baking tray. Bake on the middle shelf of the oven for 1 hour 10 minutes. Leave to cool on the tray before turning out on to a board.

Slice the cooled millet into 4 slices. Serve each topped with a good helping of smoked salmon, a dollop of crème fraîche, a sprinkling of dill and lemon wedges to squeeze over. Finish with freshly ground black pepper.

TREATS

Rye, Cacao and Cardamom Tart with Almond Custard and Berries

This tart is mega. Together rye, cacao and cardamom make an incredibly rich and satisfyingly deep-coloured pastry crust. The custard is delicious, light and softly sweet by comparison, topped with heaps of seasonal fruit. Here I've used summer berries but you could make this in autumn with blackberries and plums, or add persimmons and blood oranges for a winter tart. The tart is served cold and is almost better made a day in advance. Top with the fruit just before serving with some fresh mint tea.

FOR THE PASTRY

140g rye flour, plus extra
    for dusting
85g raw cacao powder
150g coconut palm sugar
½ teaspoon sea salt
Seeds from 10 cardamom pods,
    ground in a mortar and pestle
250g chilled unsalted butter,
    diced
1 medium egg, beaten
¼ teaspoon vanilla extract

FOR THE CUSTARD

4 medium eggs
1 tablespoon ground almonds
Pinch of sea salt
700ml unsweetened almond milk
200ml coconut cream
8 tablespoons maple syrup
Pinch of freshly ground nutmeg
1 teaspoon vanilla extract

TO SERVE

75g raspberries
75g strawberries
50g redcurrants

• Make the pastry first by combining the rye flour, cacao powder, sugar, salt and ground cardamom seeds in a food processor or blender. Add the diced butter and pulse a few times until the mixture looks like coarse breadcrumbs. Add the egg and vanilla and pulse again until it starts to come together. Tip into a bowl and push together to make a ball, then wrap in cling film and chill in the fridge for 1 hour.

Dust a work surface with a little rye flour and roll out the dough to a circle about 5mm thick, then use to line a 24cm loose-bottomed tart tin, pushing it into the edges and leaving a little pastry hanging over the edge. Prick the base a couple of times with a fork, then place in the freezer for 15 minutes to firm up. Preheat the oven to 170°C/fan 150°C/340°F/gas mark 3½.

Line the pastry case with baking paper and fill with baking beans, then bake in the oven for 25 minutes before removing the paper and beans and returning to the oven for a further 15 minutes, or until firm and dry to the touch. Set aside to cool.

•——→

Meanwhile, make the custard. Whisk together the eggs, ground almonds and salt in a large bowl and set aside for a moment. Place the almond milk and coconut cream in a pan over a medium heat and gently warm through; when you can see that it's about to boil, remove from the heat and slowly whisk into the eggs, then stir in the maple syrup, nutmeg and vanilla and leave to cool a little.

Pour the custard into the cooled pastry case and bake for 20–25 minutes until the custard starts to firm up but still has a slight wobble in the middle. Leave to cool completely before topping with the fresh berries and serving.

Oatcakes

MAKES 12–16

250g rolled oats, plus extra
  for dusting
½ teaspoon bicarbonate of soda
1 teaspoon sea salt
25g unsalted butter, at room
  temperature, chopped

I make oatcakes purely to eat cheese. Our shop in Covent Garden backs on to Neal's Yard Dairy, one of the best cheesemongers I've ever come across, if not *the* best. Stepping into their shop is dangerous for me: it's all too easy to end up buying enough cheese for 12, when I'm only meant to be buying for half that number. I love a good cheese biscuit but have found that making my own oatcakes is even better: the combination of sweet oats, butter and sea salt is a satisfyingly simple accompaniment to any good cheese. Try these with a little Nut Butter (see page 240) and honey for a sweet alternative.

• Preheat the oven to 180°C/fan 160°C/350°F/gas mark 4 and line a baking tray with baking paper.

Mix together the oats, bicarbonate of soda and salt in a large bowl. Add the butter and use your fingers to rub it in into the dry ingredients until the mixture resembles breadcrumbs. Pour in 150ml of hot water and mix until the ingredients come together into a soft dough.

Sprinkle some extra rolled oats on a cool, clean work surface and roll out the dough to a thickness of no more than 5mm. Use a cookie cutter or glass to stamp out oatcakes and transfer them to the lined baking tray (or you could cut them freehand with a knife). Bake in the oven for 20–25 minutes, or until golden. Transfer to a wire rack to cool (they will crisp up a little as they cool).

Caraway, Oat and Seed Crispbread

270g rolled oats
315g mixed seeds, such as
   sunflower, pumpkin, flaxseeds,
   sesame seeds
2 tablespoons caraway seeds
2 tablespoons chia seeds
1 teaspoon garlic flakes
2 teaspoons sea salt
3 tablespoons coconut oil,
   melted
1 tablespoon maple syrup

This is one of my favourite recipes in the book. I think it's because I'm both a garlic and a caraway addict. Caraway is amazing, it works in sweet and savoury dishes, which is why it harmonises so well with the sweetness of oats and maple syrup in this crispbread. Garlic is something I couldn't live without and makes these crackers a perfect pairing to any dip, cheese or smoked fish.

• Preheat the oven to 180°C/fan 160°C/350°F/gas mark 4 and line 2 baking trays with baking paper.

Blitz 120g of the rolled oats in a food processor until you have a coarse flour, then add to a large mixing bowl with the remaining rolled oats, all the seeds, garlic and salt and mix until combined.

Mix together the wet ingredients in a small jug with 375ml of water, add to the dry ingredients and stir until everything is nicely mixed.

Put half the mixture into the centre of one of the baking trays and lay another piece of baking paper on top. Roll out the mixture to a thickness of about 5mm, then remove the sheet of baking paper and repeat for the other batch.

Place both trays in the oven for 15–20 minutes until golden on top, then flip the crispbreads over, and return to the oven for a further 15 minutes, swapping the position of the baking trays to ensure an even bake. Leave to cool and then break into shards before eating.

Dark Chocolate, Hazelnut and Cinnamon Cookies

A warm, salted chocolate biscuit with a cup of tea is one of the best ways to get through a long, cold afternoon. These crunchy biscuits are quick and easy to bake, so make a double batch and give some to friends or little ones – everyone will want one of these, if not two. For something a little more festive, try adding the grated zest of half an unwaxed orange to the mix.

• MAKES 12

200g rolled oats
1–2 teaspoons ground cinnamon
¼ teaspoon sea salt
80g hazelnuts, crushed
50g dark chocolate, chopped
  into small chunks
2 tablespoons coconut oil,
  melted
4 tablespoons maple syrup
1 medium egg, beaten

• Preheat the oven to 180°C/fan 160°C/350°F/gas mark 4 and line a baking tray with baking paper.

Put half of the rolled oats into a food processor and blitz to a coarse flour. Tip into a large bowl along with the remaining rolled oats, the cinnamon, salt, crushed hazelnuts and chocolate chunks and mix until well combined.

Add the coconut oil, maple syrup and egg to the mixture and start to fold into the dry ingredients until you have a stiff cookie dough.

Roll portions of the dough into small walnut-sized balls in your hands. Place them on the lined baking tray, spaced well apart, and flatten them ever so slightly.

Bake in the oven for 12 minutes until golden. Leave to cool for a few minutes on the baking tray and then transfer to a wire rack to cool completely.

Drømmerkage (Dream Cake) with Blueberries

You can spot a Danish birthday party from a mile off. You'll find a group of people huddled together in a park with everything (bunting, napkins, balloons, candles) the colour and print of the red and white Danish flag. This is my version of the very traditional Danish dream cake. It's an easy cake of sponge and toasted coconut, but I assure you it will impress.

• SERVES 12–15

FOR THE CAKE

175g coconut oil, melted,
   plus extra for the tin
150g coconut palm sugar
275g rolled oats, blitzed in a food
   processor to a coarse flour
2 teaspoons baking powder
1½ teaspoons sea salt
180ml Oat Milk (see page 234)
4 medium eggs
Seeds from 1 vanilla pod, or
   1 teaspoon vanilla extract
400g blueberries

FOR THE COCONUT TOPPING

125g toasted coconut flakes,
   roughly blitzed to a slightly
   finer consistency
25g coconut oil
75g coconut palm sugar
45ml Oat Milk (see page 234)
Pinch of sea salt

• Preheat the oven to 180°C/fan 160°C/350°F/gas mark 4. Grease and line a 20cm loose-bottomed cake tin with baking paper.

Place the sugar, oats, baking powder and salt in a large bowl and stir to combine. In a separate bowl or jug, whisk together the coconut oil, oat milk, eggs and vanilla. Pour the wet ingredients into the dry and stir until completely combined.

Pour half the batter into the prepared cake tin and then scatter the blueberries across the top before adding the remaining batter. Bake in the oven for 35–40 minutes, or until a skewer inserted into the centre comes out clean.

While the cake is in the oven make the coconut topping. Toast the coconut in a dry pan over a medium heat, stirring continuously until half the coconut has turned golden brown, then remove from the pan and put to one side. Melt the coconut oil in a pan over a low heat and stir in the sugar until dissolved. Add the oat milk, whisking until smooth, then immediately stir in the coconut flakes and a big pinch of salt. Put to one side until the cake comes out of the oven.

Once the cake is just cooked, spoon over the coconut topping, pressing it over the top of the cake with the back of a spoon. Leave to cool in the tin for a few minutes before removing from the tin and serving slightly warm.

Quinoa, Plum and Cardamom Frangipane Pudding

I could tell when the summer holidays were coming to an end when my mum starting baking her buttery plum pie slices. She made little sponge pillows for the fruits – when baked, the sponge grows sweeter while the plums caramelise on top and become tart in the middle. This is my version of her pie. I adore the earthiness of the quinoa set against the plums and the maple syrup. I like to bake it in a rectangular tin so everyone can get a little half-plum square of their own.

- SERVES 12–15

300g unsalted butter,
   at room temperature,
   plus extra for the tin
150g quinoa flakes
150g ground almonds
Seeds from 20 cardamom
   pods, ground in a mortar
   and pestle
1½ teaspoons sea salt
200ml maple syrup
Seeds from 1 vanilla pod
3 medium eggs, beaten
6 plums, halved and pitted
Crème fraîche, to serve
   (optional)

- Preheat the oven to 180°C/fan 160°C/350°F/gas mark 4. Grease and line a small brownie tin, about 25 × 20cm.

Beat together the butter, quinoa, almonds, cardamom seeds, salt, maple syrup and vanilla until well combined. Beat in the eggs, one at a time, until nicely incorporated.

Pour the batter into the prepared tin and top with the plums, cut sides up, gently pushing them into the frangipane. Bake for 45–50 minutes, or until golden and a skewer inserted into the centre comes out clean.

Leave to cool completely in the tin, then cut into squares and serve with a good dollop of crème fraîche.

Yogurt Cake with Prune and Fennel Compote

Yogurt in a cake is amazing. It keeps it fresh, soft and ever so slightly tart and, well, yogurty. The prune and fennel compote adds just the right amount of sweetness.

• SERVES 8–10

100g unsalted butter,
    at room temperature
250ml maple syrup
1 tablespoon vanilla extract
Finely grated zest of
    1 unwaxed lemon
3 medium eggs, separated
250ml Greek-style yogurt
90g rolled oats, blitzed in a food
    processor to a coarse flour
100g ground almonds
80g spelt flour
1 teaspoon baking powder
½ teaspoon sea salt
150g dates, pitted and chopped

FOR THE COMPOTE
250g prunes, chopped
2 teaspoons fennel seeds
2 tablespoons maple syrup
Finely grated zest and juice
    of 1 unwaxed lemon

• Preheat the oven to 180°C/fan 160°C/350°F/gas mark 4. Line a 22cm springform cake tin with baking paper.

Place the butter, maple syrup, vanilla and lemon zest in a food processor and whizz until smooth and creamy. Add the egg yolks and yogurt and whizz again until just incorporated. Combine the oat flour, ground almonds, spelt flour, baking powder and salt in a large bowl, then stir in the wet ingredients and fold everything together until well combined.

Beat the egg whites in a separate bowl with a hand-held whisk until soft peaks form. Slowly fold the egg whites into the mixture, followed by the chopped dates. Pour the batter into the prepared tin and bake in the oven for 50–60 minutes, or until dark and golden on the top and a skewer inserted into the middle comes out clean. Remove from the oven and leave to cool for a while before lifting out the tin.

While the cake is in the oven, put all the ingredients for the compote in a pan over a medium heat with 750ml of water. Bring to the boil, then reduce the heat and simmer until it becomes jammy: 5–10 minutes. Allow to cool slightly before serving with slices of the yogurt cake, or spread the compote over the cake if you prefer.

Rosehip and Apple Crumble

Around Copenhagen at the end of the summer rosehips grow aplenty, and we'd eat them in porridges and jams until the season's harvest had been fully consumed. In London, I spot little gluts of them here and there around the end of September and early October and was determined to find my own recipe for them. They can be fiddly to prepare, but their sweet citrus kick is worth it. Make this as an alternative to your usual apple crumble. If you can't find rosehips, do still give the unusual quinoa crumble topping a try.

• SERVES 4

100g rosehips, topped and tailed,
  halved and seeds removed
175g eating apples, peeled, cored
  and roughly chopped
50g coconut palm sugar
3 tablespoons coconut oil
Juice of ½ lemon
Seeds from ½ vanilla pod
  or ½ teaspoon vanilla extract

FOR THE CRUMBLE TOPPING
100g quinoa flakes
1–2 tablespoons coconut oil,
  melted
3 tablespoons maple syrup

• Preheat the oven to 170°C/fan 150°C/340°F/gas mark 3½.

Place the rosehips, apples, sugar, coconut oil, lemon juice and vanilla into a pan and place over a medium heat, stirring together until the edges of the apple start to turn golden, about 8 minutes. Add 65ml of water and continue to cook for another 10–15 minutes until the fruit is soft and the water has reduced down to a couple of tablespoons.

Meanwhile mix together the quinoa flakes, coconut oil and maple syrup until well combined and spread out on a baking tray. Bake in the oven for 20 minutes, stirring after 10 minutes.

Divide the apple compote between 4 plates and top each with a good helping of crumble. This is delicious served warm with a little cream or crème fraîche.

Fig and Lavender Parfait with Cacao and Hazelnut Granola

• SERVES 2

FOR THE GRANOLA
100g buckwheat groats,
   soaked in water for 1 hour
3 tablespoons olive oil
3 tablespoons maple syrup
2 teaspoons raw cacao powder
3 tablespoons skinned hazelnuts

FOR THE PARFAIT
1 tablespoon honey
1 lavender flower or ½ teaspoon
   dried lavender
Seeds from ½ vanilla pod
160ml coconut yogurt
4 figs, roughly chopped

I've learned a lot about figs in recent years. Dom's family have a few fig trees in their garden in France and they become wonderfully uncontrollable in the late summer months. We have made fig purée, dried figs, fig ice cream and fig chutney – this recipe was another of our figgy adventures. I love the floral hint of the lavender, the creaminess of the coconut and, of course, the simple treasure of fresh figs at the bottom of this parfait. This can easily be made ahead and left to chill in the fridge.

• Rinse and drain the buckwheat groats and leave to dry out completely.

Preheat the oven to 180°C/fan 160°C/350°F/gas mark 4 and line a baking tray with baking paper. Make the granola first by mixing the buckwheat groats, olive oil, maple syrup, cacao and hazelnuts together until well combined. Transfer to the lined tray and bake for 30–40 minutes until crisp, checking and stirring it every 10 minutes. Leave to cool.

Place the honey, lavender and ½ teaspoon of water in a small pan and warm over a low heat for a couple of minutes to make a lavender honey. Remove the lavender, and set aside to cool.

Gradually whisk the lavender honey and vanilla seeds into the coconut yogurt until it becomes light and fluffy. Layer up each serving with the chopped figs, coconut yogurt and cacao granola.

Cardamom Affogato

• SERVES 4–6

400ml Oat Milk (see page 234)
200ml oat cream (see page 234)
Seeds from ½ vanilla pod
Seeds from 5 cardamom pods,
    ground in a mortar and pestle
65ml maple syrup
4–6 shots of good-quality
    hot espresso (or use strong
    cafetière coffee)
Dark chocolate shavings,
    to serve

I put this recipe in to tell my sister's favourite joke:

Vicky: What's that pudding I really like?
Me: Give me a hint.
Vicky: You know, the vanilla ice cream with an espresso
shot poured over the top?
Me: Affogato?
Vicky: Yes! Affogato what it's called. Thanks.

Simple recipe, even simpler joke; both very enjoyable.

• Put the oat milk, oat cream, vanilla seeds and cardamom seeds
in a pan and place over a low heat. Remove from the heat
just before it comes to the boil and stir in the maple syrup.
Allow to cool.

Pour the cooled mixture into a 500ml plastic container and
freeze for at least 4 hours, preferably overnight. Once it is
completely frozen, remove from the freezer, transfer the
mixture to a blender and blitz until smooth (you may need to
do this in batches). Return to the container and freeze again
for another hour. This process is to break up the ice crystals
and will give your ice cream a creamier consistency.

Add a scoop or two of the cardamom ice cream to small
glasses or bowls. Pour a shot of hot fresh espresso or coffee
over each serving and top with shaved dark chocolate.
Serve with a teaspoon and eat immediately.

How to Build Porridge Bread

I hate anything going to waste, and luckily with porridge it doesn't have to. This is a simple, quick recipe – if you have any leftover porridge at breakfast, you'll have a fresh loaf by lunchtime. Be as creative as you like with your porridge and then the flavour, spices and sweetness will come through in your bread.

- **MAKES 1 LARGE LOAF**

400g strong wholemeal bread flour, plus extra for dusting
1 tablespoon sea salt
7g fast-action yeast
200g leftover porridge, cooled
2 tablespoons olive oil

- Sift the flour into a mixing bowl and add the sea salt and yeast, making sure they're well combined. Create a small well in the middle of the flour mix and add the porridge and 250ml of lukewarm water. Start folding the flour into the middle, gradually working the mixture into a dough; it will be fairly soft. Cover with a damp tea towel and leave to rest for 1 hour, until it has doubled in size.

Spread some flour on a cool, clean work surface and tip the dough out on to it. Knead the dough by pushing the heel of your hand into the middle of the dough, stretching it out, folding it in and then giving the dough a quarter turn and repeating. This doesn't need to be done for long – just until the dough is even and elastic.

Drizzle the olive oil over the outside of the dough as you begin to shape your loaf. I do this by tucking my fingers ever so slightly under the edges of the dough and spinning it clockwise to create a nice, round loaf. Cover the shaped dough with the same damp tea towel and leave it to prove for 40 minutes; it will expand by about one third. Meanwhile preheat the oven to 220°C/fan 200°C/425°F/gas mark 7 and lightly flour a baking tray.

Move the dough from the work surface to the middle of the baking tray. Bake for 10 minutes, then reduce the oven temperature to 180°C/fan 160°C/350°F/gas mark 4 for a further 30–35 minutes. Leave to cool slightly before slicing.

How to Turn
Porridge into Pancakes

This easy recipe shows you how to transform any leftover porridge into delicious pancakes. You might have chosen to add spices, flavours or additional grains to your porridge that you wouldn't have tried in a pancake and can therefore create a whole new collection of recipes. Some of my favourites have been cacao and coconut oil, carrot and banana and lemon and poppy seed.

- SERVES 2

100g leftover porridge, cooled
100g rolled oats
2 medium eggs, separated
Pinch of sea salt
1 teaspoon baking powder
1 teaspoon vanilla extract
2 tablespoons juice/milk/ nut milk
4 teaspoons coconut oil or unsalted butter, for frying

TO SERVE
Maple syrup, fruit, yogurt, seeds

- Make the batter by combining the leftover porridge, rolled oats, eggs yolks, salt, baking powder, vanilla extract and your choice of liquid in a food processor and whizz for a minute until fully combined.

In a separate bowl, whisk the egg whites to stiff peaks, then fold into the pancake batter.

Place a large frying pan over medium heat and melt the coconut oil or butter. Pour most of it into a bowl or cup to use to grease the pan for the rest of the pancakes (you'll be cooking these in batches).

Spoon 2 tablespoons of batter into the hot pan, swirl the pan a little to spread the batter and then add another 2 tablespoons and swirl again. Cook for 2 minutes until golden on the bottom and bubbles start to appear on the surface, then flip and cook the other side for another few minutes. Keep warm while you cook the rest of the pancakes, adding a little melted coconut oil or butter each time. Serve with maple syrup, fruit, yogurt, seeds or any topping that takes your fancy.

VARIATION
Fold a handful of blueberries or some chopped banana into the batter with the egg whites, or scatter over the uncooked surface of the pancake so that they sink into the batter while the underside cooks.

Lemon and Honey Oat Panna Cotta

I can't resist a panna cotta and get so excited by the prospect of pairing it with fruits such as rhubarb or blood orange. But really, the very best panna cotta is a refreshing and light lemony version. This recipe is easy to make and works beautifully every time. You can either serve it in your favourite bowls or turn it out onto a plate.

• MAKES 4

250ml Oat Milk (see page 234)
250ml oat cream
Finely grated zest of
   2 unwaxed lemons
Seeds from ½ vanilla pod
2 teaspoons gelatine (look for
   grass-fed gelatine if possible)
3 tablespoons honey

• Combine the oat milk and oat cream in a pan with the lemon zest and vanilla. Slowly bring to the boil (keeping an eye on it), then take off the heat just as it starts to simmer.

Put the gelatine in a bowl, pour in 4 tablespoons of the hot milk/cream mixture and allow to 'bloom' (soften). Set the remaining milk/cream mixture aside to infuse and cool.

Once the milk/cream mixture has cooled, stir it into the gelatine and add the honey. Strain into a jug, then pour into 4 ramekins or bowls. Place in the fridge to chill and set for at least 4 hours.

Once the panna cottas are set and you're ready to serve, briefly dip the base of each of the chilled ramekins into a bowl of hot water and then run a blunt knife around the edge. Place a serving plate on top, then turn each panna cotta out on to a plate. Serve with some fresh fruit or a ginger biscuit.

Puffed Quinoa Treats

A crispy, crunchy light treat, this easy recipe is great for an afternoon snack or as a little pudding. You can use a number of different puffed grains here: amaranth, buckwheat or rice would all work well. You can find puffed grains in some specialist stores or online but you can also puff them yourself. They won't pop quite as much as the ones you'll find in the shop, as producers use a process of compression before popping, but it's fun to make your own at home.

COCONUT, HONEY AND GINGER

- MAKES 12

4 tablespoons honey
4 tablespoons coconut oil
1 tablespoon grated root ginger
100g puffed quinoa
1 tablespoon toasted coconut flakes

- Line a 12-hole muffin tray with paper cases. (Or make your own from squares of baking paper, see page 86.) Mix the honey, coconut oil and ginger together in a bowl. Add the puffed quinoa and coconut flakes and stir until thoroughly coated. Spoon into the paper cases and chill in the fridge for 20 minutes to set.

PEANUT, CACAO AND HONEY

- MAKES 12

4 tablespoons honey
5 tablespoons peanut butter
  (unsalted if possible, for
  homemade see page 240)
Pinch of sea salt
100g puffed quinoa
2 tablespoon cacao nibs
4 tablespoons coconut oil

- Line a 12-hole muffin tray with paper cases. (Or make your own from squares of baking paper, see page 86.) Mix the honey, peanut butter and salt together in a bowl (if you can't find unsalted peanut butter you may want to leave out the salt). Add the puffed quinoa and cacao nibs and stir until thoroughly coated. Spoon into the paper cases and chill in the fridge for 20 minutes to set. You can also pour the mixture into tins, and serve as a slice.

Oat Milk and
Raspberry Popsicles

MAKES 8

400ml Oat Milk (see page 234)
200ml oat cream (see page 234)
Seeds from ½ vanilla pod
Juice from ½ lemon
65ml maple syrup
150g raspberries

I urge you to buy a popsicle mould for this recipe. They are fun to play with and easy to use and you'll always be pleased with the result. For me, a popsicle after a swim on a hot day at the height of summer is pure bliss. These little ice creams feel very indulgent, because oats are so silky and creamy. Prepare these pops the night before to make sure they're ready for the following day. Try throwing in some other berries, or perhaps granola or cacao nibs at the base for a little crunch.

- Mix the oat milk, oat cream, lemon juice and vanilla seeds together in a pan and warm gently over a low heat, removing from the heat just before it comes to the boil. Stir in the maple syrup.

  Pour into your popsicle mould, filling not quite to the top to leave room for the raspberries. Drop the raspberries in and poke them down and around so they're evenly distributed. Place in the freezer for at least 4 hours, or ideally overnight.

  •⟶

Cinnamon Baked Pineapple
with Amaranth Cream

• SERVES 4

100g whole amaranth, soaked
   in water for 1 hour
400ml can of coconut milk
2 tablespoons maple syrup
½ teaspoon sea salt
½ ripe pineapple, peeled
   and cut into 1cm slices
1 teaspoon ground cinnamon
2 tablespoons coconut oil,
   for frying
Pistachio nuts, chopped,
   to serve

The pineapple in this recipe starts to caramelise instantly
and becomes sticky and sweeter when cooked with a little
cinnamon and coconut oil. My favourite way to cook it is
to put the wrapped pineapple over the dying embers of a
barbecue, turning it every so often. The amaranth adds
a wonderfully light texture and nuttiness to the dish, making
it incredibly moreish (you might want to make extra).

• Rinse and drain the amaranth and place in a pan with the coconut
   milk, maple syrup and salt. Cook over a medium heat for 45 minutes
   until thickened, then set aside.

Meanwhile put the pineapple into a shallow bowl and dust with
the cinnamon until all the pieces have a good coating. Melt the
coconut oil in a frying pan over a medium heat and fry the
pineapple slices for 4 minutes on each side until the edges start
to caramelise.

Transfer the cooked amaranth with its cooking liquid to a food
processor or blender and blitz until just a little coarse.

You can serve this dish hot or cold, they're both equally delicious.
Pour the amaranth cream into a bowl and top with the cinnamon
pineapple and pistachio nuts.

Cacao and Rye Rolls

These little rolls are great at any time of day. I like them in the afternoon, dipping them into a cup of coffee, or with a little salted butter or nut butter. You can also make them with a good crack of black pepper and serve them with cheese or as a picnic bun with cucumber and salad – delicious.

- MAKES 24

4 teaspoons fast-action yeast
750g rye flour
250g spelt flour
4 tablespoons raw cacao powder
4 teaspoons sea salt
200ml maple syrup
6 tablespoons olive oil, plus
  more for greasing
2 medium egg whites,
  lightly beaten
100g cocoa nibs

- Activate the yeast first by placing it in small bowl or cup and covering it with 150ml of lukewarm water. Place somewhere warm for 10–15 minutes until a light froth has formed on the surface.

Place both the flours, the cacao powder and salt in a very large mixing bowl. Make a well in the centre and add the yeast mixture, maple syrup and olive oil. Using your hands, start to bring the mixture together. Slowly start adding 375–400ml of cold water, mixing until you have a rough dough. Turn out the dough onto a lightly oiled work surface and knead it for 10–15 minutes, or until the dough is smooth and shiny. Place the dough into an oiled bowl, cover with a tea towel and leave to rise for at least 1 hour, or until doubled in size.

Remove the risen dough from the mixing bowl and knead for another 30 seconds, to knock the air out of it. Divide the dough into 24 equal-sized portions. Roll each portion into a tight ball, and place on a baking tray. Once all balls have been rolled, leave to prove for another hour. Towards the end of the proving time, preheat the oven to 220°C/fan 200°C/425°F/gas mark 7 and line a baking tray with baking paper.

Once the rolls have proved, place a large roasting tin on the bottom shelf of the oven and half-fill it with hot water to create steam. Place the egg whites in one bowl and the cocoa nibs in another. Dip each roll in the egg white, then toss in the cacao nibs before placing on the lined baking tray. Bake in the middle of the oven for 20–25 minutes, turning the baking tray around halfway through to ensure an even bake. Remove from the oven and leave to cool before serving.

LARDER

Oat Milk

This is simple to make, delicious and versatile – I use it in endless recipes – from porridge and spiced hot drinks to panna cotta and ice cream – pretty much anywhere you would use milk. By using half the amount of water you can create oat cream, which is a great dairy-free alternative for quiches and pasta sauces. This recipe takes no time to make; all you need is a fine strainer, such as a muslin cloth or nut milk bag, for the blended mix.

- **MAKES 1 LITRE**

100g rolled oats, soaked in
   water for at least 30 minutes
900ml filtered water
Pinch of sea salt
1 teaspoon vanilla extract
   (optional)

- Rinse and drain the oats thoroughly and then put into a blender with all the remaining ingredients. Blitz until the oats are completely blended.

   Set a fine strainer lined with a muslin cloth, or a nut milk bag, over a bowl and pour the oat mixture into it, squeezing to get all the liquid into the bowl. Decant into a clean bottle and store in the fridge for 3–4 days.

Barley Tea

55g pearl barley

Barley tea is a new thing for me. I first read about it when one of the characters from a book by Japanese author Haruki Murakami sipped on his barley tea and leaned back against the fridge to gather his thoughts. I was immediately curious about what this protagonist was enjoying and what part it plays in everyday Japanese culture. It turns out it is incredibly simple to make and tastes delicious and savoury – similar to a roasted corn kernel. It is also praised for its health benefits and is rich in antioxidants. I keep mine simple, iced if it's a warm day and sometimes with a lick of honey.

- Rinse the barley well in a sieve under cold water. Set aside and allow to dry fully, or tip onto a clean tea towel and gently rub dry.

Place a pan over a medium heat and leave it for a minute or so to get really hot, with the heat spread evenly over the base of the pan. Test the pan is hot enough by adding a drop of water: if it sizzles immediately, it is ready.

Add the barley and toast it in the pan until a deep golden brown, about 7–8 minutes, stirring continuously.

To make a mug of tea, add 1 tablespoon of the toasted barley to 250ml of boiling water (or add 3 tablespoons to a teapot and add 750ml of boiling water). For a little sweetness, add 1 teaspoon of honey.

Chia Jams

Who would have thought that making jam could be such a simple process, without the need for a sack of sugar? Chia is remarkably versatile and can be used in all sorts of puddings as it works as a wonderful thickener. Those little seeds swell enormously and give the jam its jelly-ness without the need for pectin. You can try this with any variety of fruits depending on the season and experiment with your own assortment of spices. Just be mindful of how watery the fruit is that you're starting with and alter the amount of water that you add each time (you can always add more if it's a little stodgy). Of course, you can also add more chia seeds if it's a little soupy.

RASPBERRY FENNEL JAM

- MAKES 1–2 JARS

500g raspberries
4 tablespoons honey
5 tablespoons chia seeds
Juice of ¼ lemon
½ teaspoon fennel seeds

- Place the raspberries in a food processor or blender and blitz for a few seconds until you have a purée. Tip into a bowl and add all the remaining ingredients with 2 tablespoons of water. Stir well, then leave for 10 minutes to allow the chia seeds to expand and thicken the jam.

Transfer the jam to a sterilised jar or jars with tight-fitting lids and store in the fridge for up to 7 days. Use as you would regular jam – on bread, yogurt and porridge and in desserts.

MULBERRY JAM

- MAKES 1–2 JARS

500g mulberries, washed and stalks picked off
4 tablespoons honey
5 tablespoons chia seeds
Juice of ¼ lemon

- Put the mulberries, honey and 2 tablespoons of water in a pan and place over a medium heat for about 4–5 minutes until the mulberries have softened and started to break down (you may want to mash them lightly with a fork). Remove from the heat.

Add the chia seeds and lemon juice and leave for 10 minutes to allow the chia seeds to expand.

Transfer the jam to a sterilised jar or jars with tight-fitting lids and store in the fridge for up to 7 days.

The best way to sterilise your jars is to wash them with warm soapy water, thoroughly, then place them in a low-temperature oven (around 110°C/fan 100°C/230°F/ gas mark ½) for at least 20 minutes.

BLOOD ORANGE MARMALADE

• MAKES 1 JAR

500g unwaxed blood oranges
   (about 3-4 oranges)
4 tablespoons honey
5 tablespoons chia seeds
Juice of ¼ lemon
½ teaspoon ground spice,
   such as cinnamon, cardamom
   or ginger (optional)

• Finely grate the zest of the oranges into a pan and then use a sharp knife to remove all the white pith from the oranges. (Do this over the pan to catch the juices). Now cut the oranges into segments. Add the orange segments to the pan with the honey and 100ml of water. Place over a medium heat for about 4–5 minutes to soften the oranges (use a fork to break them up).

Remove from the heat and add the chia seeds, lemon juice and spice, if using. Leave for 10 minutes to allow the chia seeds to expand.

Once cool, transfer the marmalade to a sterilised jar with a tight-fitting lid and store in the fridge for up to 7 days.

Sugars and Maples

I love playing with different sweeteners and spices. I lived in America until I was eight and, every Sunday, my dad would get up early with all five of us kids, pile us in the car and take us for pancakes. My order was always a short stack with a side of bacon. It was there that I was first introduced to blueberry maple syrup – a sickly blue mess that came in a plastic dispenser that appealed to my eight-year-old sensibilities. I'm still partial to maple syrup as a sweetener, as it packs a punch even in small amounts and has a ton of nutritional benefits, including zinc and manganese. Grains have their own flavours, of course, but it's nice to layer on top of them, too. Here are some of my favourites – any of these maple syrups or sugars would taste delicious on porridge or drizzled over pancakes, on yogurt, ice creams or puddings. You could even use them in a drink to sweeten a lemonade or tea.

LAVENDER MAPLE SYRUP
365ml pure maple syrup
1 tablespoon dried lavender

CARDAMOM MAPLE SYRUP
365ml pure maple syrup
Seeds from 7 cardamom pods, crushed in a mortar and pestle

GINGER MAPLE SYRUP
365ml pure maple syrup
1 tablespoon finely
    chopped fresh ginger

BLUEBERRY MAPLE
365ml pure maple syrup
2 tablespoons crushed blueberries

- Put the maple syrup, 2 tablespoons of water and the flowers, spices or fruit in a pan and place over a medium heat. Bring slowly to the boil and remove from the heat once it starts to bubble. Allow to cool completely to allow the flavours to infuse.

Once cool, strain the maple syrup through a fine sieve into a container and discard the flowers, spices or fruit. (You can leave them in if you really want a flavour-hit.) Store in the fridge for up to 2 weeks.

CINNAMON COCONUT PALM SUGAR
100g coconut palm sugar
2 tablespoons ground cinnamon

LIQUORICE COCONUT PALM SUGAR
100g coconut palm sugar
2 tablespoons ground liquorice root

- Add the coconut palm sugar and ground spices to a mixing bowl and mix well. Store in a jar with a tight-fitting lid (it will keep indefinitely).

TARRAGON COCONUT PALM SUGAR
100g coconut palm sugar
Small handful of tarragon leaves

- Blitz the coconut palm sugar and tarragon in a blender until the herb has broken down and the sugar takes on the texture of slightly wet sand. Store in a jar with a tight-fitting lid in the fridge for up to 7 days.

Nut Butters

Nut butter and apple, nut butter and steamed greens, nut butter and fresh bread... I think most dishes would work well with nut butter – my housemate even likes it with hash browns. Making nut butter is so easy and infinitely worthwhile, both in terms of flavour and cost, although it helps to have a good-quality food processor or blender. It's also a moment to get creative, play with different nuts, add some heat or perhaps some cacao. And as the nuts roast, their warming scent wafts around the house. Be warned: hungry people will fast approach.

- MAKES 300G

300g nuts, such as peanuts, almonds, hazelnuts, cashews, pecan nuts, pistachios
Pinch of sea salt (optional)

- Preheat the oven to 160°C/fan 140°C/325°F/gas mark 3.

Spread the nuts out on a baking tray and roast on the middle shelf of the oven for 15–20 minutes until they become fragrant and golden.

Tip the nuts into a food processor or blender and blitz for a minute or so to break them down. Scrape down the sides and then blitz again at the highest setting. The nuts will start to clump together and eventually, as the nut oils are released, a smooth paste will form. Depending on the power of your blender, this could take 8–14 minutes. Add the salt a minute before the end, if using. I have found that a food processor with wide base works better for nut butter, but you can still make it in a smoothie blender; it just might take a little longer.

FLAVOURING
IDEAS

Add any of the following flavourings to the nut butter mix above, either at the final stages of blending or simply stirred into the butter before placing in a jar.

Be careful not to over-blend the nuts as they can start to become thick and clumpy. If this happens, you can always add a little coconut or other oil to loosen it back to your preferred texture.

Transfer to a clean jar and store in the fridge for up to 2 weeks.

SRIRACHA NUT BUTTER
Add 3 tablespoons of Sriracha hot sauce – perfect with steamed greens or chicken.

CACAO AND SEA SALT NUT BUTTER
Add 1 tablespoon of raw cacao powder and ½ teaspoon of sea salt.

CHAI SPICED NUT BUTTER
Add 1 tablespoon of Chai Spice (see page 242).

Yogurt Alternatives

Yogurt is instantly refreshing, whether it's with some crunchy granola and fresh berries on a summer morning or used to top a bowl of porridge in the middle of winter. I've recently started to think of other ways to create that same cool contrast with some of my favourite ingredients. Here are some dairy-free 'yogurt' alternatives.

NUT 'YOGURT'

- SERVES 2

145g nuts (cashews, almonds
    or hazelnuts), soaked in
    water for 6 hours or overnight
4 medjool dates, pitted
¼ teaspoon sea salt

- Rinse and drain the soaked nuts and put them in a blender with 500ml water, the dates and salt. Blitz on high speed until completely smooth and yogurt-like in consistency. Depending on how thick you like your yogurt, feel free to add a little more water to make it slightly runnier. Pour into a bowl and top with fresh or dried fruit, nuts, seeds or granola.

MANGO BANANA 'YOGURT'

- SERVES 1–2

1 banana
1 mango, peeled and stoned
Juice of ½ lime
Seeds from ½ vanilla pod
1 teaspoon honey (optional)

- Add the banana, mango, lime juice and vanilla to a blender and blitz until smooth. If you want to add a little sweetness to your yogurt, add honey. Pour into a bowl and top with fresh or dried fruit, nuts, seeds or granola.

Spices for Drinks

There is nothing like wrapping your hands around a hot, spiced drink in the middle of winter. These recipes use some of my favourite spices, which are seen in a lot in Danish cooking. The combination of cinnamon, cardamom, ginger and cloves in the Chai Spice reminds me of cold, dark winter nights; my spirits were immediately lifted. The smell of those spices and the memories sum up perfectly the idea of *hygge*.

CHAI SPICE

5 tablespoons ground cardamom
2 tablespoons ground cinnamon
½ tablespoon ground cloves
1½ tablespoons ground ginger
Good grinding of black pepper
½ tablespoon freshly grated nutmeg
40g coconut palm sugar

- Mix all the ingredients together and store in a jar in a cool, dry place for several months (most spices deteriorate after a year).

To make a chai spiced drink, mix 1 teaspoon of the spice blend with 250ml milk of your choice and heat gently, stirring continuously.

TURMERIC SPICE

5 tablespoons ground turmeric
5 tablespoons ground cinnamon
Good grinding of black pepper

- Mix all the ingredients together and store in a jar in a cool dry place for several months.

To make a turmeric spiced drink, mix ½ teaspoon of the spice blend with 250ml milk of your choice and heat gently, stirring continuously.

To make a turmeric hot chocolate, mix ½ teaspoon of the spice blend with 1 teaspoon of raw cacao powder and make as above.

Basic Compote

• MAKES 2 JARS

150g fruit (see right)
1 tablespoon maple syrup
Juice of ½ lemon
Spices (optional), see right

Whenever I feel like making a fruit compote I just let myself be dictated to by what is in season. Using seasonal fruit means that it's at its best in terms of ripeness and sweetness and you can usually just let the fruit do all the work. Use the recipe below as a guide, I occasionally add spices (vanilla, cardamom, cinnamon), grated unwaxed orange zest and sometimes a pinch of sea salt. A compote makes a great porridge topping, or simply stir through yogurt.

Soft fruit and berries just need to be washed, but larger fruit such as peaches and apricots should be pitted and roughly chopped.

• Prepare the fruit (see above) and put it into a pan with the maple syrup and 1 tablespoon of water. Place over a medium heat and bring slowly to the boil. Reduce the heat to a simmer and add the lemon juice and spices, if using. Simmer for a few minutes to allow the fruit to soften and break up slightly (you may need to mash it lightly with a fork).

Remove from the heat and allow to cool. Store in the fridge until needed, for up to 5 days.

Index

Page numbers in **bold**
denote a main entry

a

b

Alex Hely-Hutchinson

Alex Hely-Hutchinson runs 26 Grains, which puts porridge on the map. 26 Grains began life as pop-up serving porridge at London's Old Street station before blossoming into a shop space in Neal's Yard, London. Find out more about what's coming up at 26grains.com and @26grains.

Alex's inspiration for 26 Grains was a year she spent in Copenhagen, where she acquired a Nordic love for ancient grains and natural flavourings, and fell for the way in which a simple bowl of porridge can inspire feelings of contentment or *hygge*. Aged 26, Alex lives in East London.

Cook's Notes

SEASONALITY   Seasonality is hugely important to the way I cook and what we serve in the shop. In addition, we try to cook with foods that haven't travelled too far. It takes a lot of patience to wait for the British berry to come into season, but it doesn't compare to anything else the rest of the year. It's exciting and engaging and I wouldn't have it any other way.

CITRUS ZESTS   Always buy unwaxed fruit if you are going to use the zests and, in any case, give them a good scrub before using. (All organic citrus fruits are also unwaxed.)

DAIRY PRODUCE AND EGGS   I always buy organic.

FISH   As the recipes in this book reflect, I eat fish little and often. I always buy sustainable, ethically-sourced fish.

GELATINE   Only one recipe in this book contains gelatine (Lemon and Honey Oat Panna Cotta, see page 220), but do try to find grass-fed gelatine, which is from healthy, well-treated cows.

MAPLE SYRUP   Try to buy pure, unadulterated syrups and always read the label. Many contain only a percentage of pure maple syrup, bulked out with factory-made syrups.

MEAT   As per the balance of this book, I don't eat meat very often. When I do, I always buy organic meat from animals that have enjoyed a good quality of life. This costs more, so I eat it less often.

NUT BUTTERS   These are easy to make yourself if you have a decent blender (see page 240). But they are also now widely available. Try to buy unsalted nut butters (read the label), especially if you are going to use them in sweet recipes.

OLIVE OIL   I used refined olive oil for baking where I do not want a strong taste to come through, for example, in cake batters. The best, expensive extra-virgin olive oils should be reserved for salad dressings; don't try to cook with them, as it damages their structure as well as spoils their flavour.

OVENS   I have given a range of temperatures for all my oven-baked recipes – Celsius, Celsius fan oven, Fahrenheit and gas mark – in order to be as reader-friendly as possible. Always make sure your oven is running at the temperature you think it is (see Thermometers, below).

PLANT-BASED MILKS   The quality of these in the shops is highly variable. Many (including the top-selling, most widely available brands) contain ingredients I haven't heard of, and often lots of sugar as well. Try to make your own if you can find the time (see page 234 for an Oat Milk I frequently use in my recipes) but, if you can't, buy unsweetened brands (read the label).

THERMOMETERS   If you think your oven may be cooler or hotter than the average, an oven thermometer is invaluable to help you calibrate the temperature and know how to get the best results. They are reasonably inexpensive. An oil thermometer is also useful for deep-frying. I don't deep-fry often but, when I do, I want the results to be crisp and amazing, not soggy and sad, which is easier to achieve when you can test the temperature of the oil.

Acknowledgements

My siblings: Victoria, for the encouragement and complete photography genius (the pictures are above and beyond what I could have ever hoped for) and for giving her unbelievable support wherever she could; Teddy, for the transport, heavy-lifting and honest criticism; Nick, for being the most efficient extra pair of hands when preparing for an event or pop-up – he truly takes direction and delivers like no one else; and Lucy, who I wish could work alongside me at the shop everyday, because when I look over at her in a moment where my head might blow she knows exactly what I'm thinking and is the best sidekick ever. Of course, I couldn't have done this without the encouragement of my parents; my Dad who consoles and manages me mentally and helps me feel confident in every decision I do or don't make, and my Mum, who I tease about not being able to cook (because she can't), who knows when I'm even more run down than I know, and is there for me when I need her without me even having to ask. And to my main man Dom, who has carried, lifted, cleaned, sold, charmed, and on occasion broken, and who has added so much to this adventure. How he has not given up because of loss of sleep from my nights of angst or excitement, the early starts and general craziness, amazes me.

Rory Buchanan, for your property advice and skills; Mark Wogan for being there for all of my endless questions; Marcos Grossi for being our guardian angel in the night; Tom Marriot for time and hard work building the shop; Tanita de Ruijit for looking out for me; Amanda Kievet for our beautiful slick logo; Rob Prentice for building our show-stopping bar; Ella Woodward for her enormous support and kindness; Hatch (Skitt and Holly) for making us feel at home and confident in your beautiful place; Appear Here for getting us in to our first space; Cathryn Summerhayes for being a hard nut and for your encouragement; Rowan Yapp for her amazing work ethic and believing in this endeavour; Linda Berlin for her unbelievable contribution to the way our food looks; Georgia Levy and Ben Benton for being the backbone in the kitchen; Sandra Zellmer for her amazing design and vision for the book; Issy Croker and Meg Abbott for being the cool cats you are, Orillo for the kindness, support and beautiful videography; Emilie Holmes for having a lot of the answers to my numerous queries; James and Rosie Ramsden who first gave me the confidence that I could ever begin to write a book; Katherine, Charlotte, Tessa, Joey, Hamish, Bella, Beth, Lydia, Elly, Molly, for your amazing contribution to the shop, you guys are awesome.

And finally, to everyone who has walked into the shop, come to our pop-ups and shared my vision, without you I wouldn't be writing this. Thank you.

1 3 5 7 9 10 8 6 4 2

Square Peg, an imprint of Vintage,
20 Vauxhall Bridge Road,
London SW1V 2SA

Square Peg is part of the Penguin Random House
group of companies whose addresses can be found
at global.penguinrandomhouse.com

Text copyright © Alex Hely-Hutchinson 2016
Photography © Victoria Hely-Hutchinson 2016

First published by Square Peg in 2016

Penguin.co.uk/vintage

A CIP catalogue record for this book is available
from the British Library

ISBN 9781910931035

Design by Sandra Zellmer
Photography by Victoria Hely-Hutchinson
Prop Styling by Linda Berlin
Food Styling by Alex Hely-Hutchinson
Kitchen Assistance by The Kitchen Cooperative
Printed and bound in Italy, by L.E.G.O. Spa

Penguin Random House is committed to a sustainable
future for our business, our readers and our planet.
This book is made from Forest Stewardship Council®
certified paper.